Out of Aloneness

OUT OF ALONENESS

Discover the Natural Flow in *Your* Movement

Using movement for a healthier and happier mind, body, and spirit

by

Jack Wiener, LP, NCPsyA, CDMT
Creative Movement Teacher, Analyst
Psychotherapist, Psychoanalyst

Jack Wiener, CMT, LP, NCPsyA
jawiener6@gmail.com

International Psychoanalytic Books (IPBooks)
New York • http://www.IPBooks.net

Out of Aloneness: Discover the Natural Flow in Your Movement

Published by IPBooks, Queens, NY
Online at: www.IPBooks.net

Copyright © 2020 Jack Wiener, LP, NCPsyA, CDMT

All rights reserved. This book may not be reproduced, transmitted, or stored, in whole or in part by any means, including graphic, electronic, or mechanical without the express permission of the author and/or publisher, except in the case of brief quotations embodied in critical articles and reviews.

ISBN: 978-1-949093-72-8

*For my mother, Sureh and my father, Heinach Viner
the nurturing earth for my most personal feelings.*

Contents

Introduction 1

1. Believing in Hope 5
   My Father and Hope 5
   Sensation Leads to Hope 8
   Circulation Is Health and Hope.................................... 13
   Choice is an Option, NOT the Solution 16

2. How Hope is Lost.. 21
   Movement, Mind, Feelings.. 21
   Dissociations, Fixations, the Senses............................. 26
   Nothing moves when the mind fixates. 27
   Mark and The Time Machine 29
   Time again... 32
   Awareness is Practical 35
   Awareness is Specific 37

3. Lost in Fear 41
   The Magical Body of Denial 41
   Denial Reversed.. 46
   Movement is the Archenemy of Terror....................... 48
   Another citing of Reversal... 53

    What Gets Reversed 55
    How the Body Splits 59

4. Awakening from Fear 71
    The Fear of Intimacy 71
    Alone, Control, Letting go.. 81
    Transitions... 83
    Certainty.. 86
    Something is Wrong?.. 92
    A Turning Point.. 93
    Our Way of Life 97

5. Practicality is Hope 103
    The Odyssey to Muscles 103
    Discoveries and Insights.. 103
    Overview 103
    In the Beginning 104
    About Children and Adults 104
    Commentary 105
    Conceptualizing Teaching 108
    Children... 109
    Commentary 120
    How available is our body?....................................... 123
    Adults 128
    Beginner's Level 131
    Intermediate Level 136
    Advanced Level – Space... 142
    Advanced Level – Time.. 145
    Evaluation 148
    The Continuing Struggle 148
    Conclusion... 149

CONTENTS

6. Practical Advice for Everyone 151
   The Only Sensitive Way to Exercise 151
   Symmetry 161
   The Flat of the Heels 163
   The most recent discovery 163
   Standing 169
   Into the World of Equals.. 169
   The 4TH Toe Line 177
   The Base for Motion 177
   Hope 183
   Walking 183
   The Call to Freedom... 183
   The Interplay of Muscles 192

7. Awareness, the Practicality of Presence 199
   PRESENCE 202
   CODA 210
   BIO 211

Acknowledgements

My father's grounded curiosity and my mother's wishful hopes continue to feed my discoveries about life.

My students, three to eighty-year-olds, have taught me to understand the many ways movement reveal or mask feelings. I remain honored by their trust and commitment. I am continually learning from their inherent sensitivity and courage.

To the Israeli master movement teacher, Aryeh Kalev whose kindness and tempered insights introduced me to a relaxation experience that eventuated in my creative-movement explorations of space and time. He has remained in my thoughts since the late fifties when we first met.

To Paul Zelevansky, conceptual artist, who has helped refine the voice I give to my thoughts. To Mike Eigen, psychoanalyst, for affirming and sharing with his worldwide community the value he sees in my considerations about the body and soul. To Bernie Berkowitz, psychoanalyst, who grasped how far-reaching the scope of my work is, calling it genius. To Elizabeth Thorne, JD, psychoanalyst, who drove me to understand the difference between solving a problem and listening to feelings. To Velleda Ciccoli, psychoanalyst, whose voice championed my work with delight and enthusiasm. To Ben Marinucci and Helene Bass-Wichelhaus, two psychoanalysts who have valued my effort to bring movement and psychoanalysis together. To Marianne Lester, who began at eighty, quickly grasped the emotional depth of the physical changes in other students resulting from my suggestions and worked privately with me until her ninety-seventh year. I am deeply grateful to my wife, Arlette. Her sense of the reader's possible reaction to a word or a thought, continually awakens my sense of who I am talking with.

Introduction

This book reveals little-known but powerful techniques that have helped countless people improve their body, enliven their mind, and spark their spirit. These techniques have caused a life-long limp to disappear, allowed a frightened and stiffening body to turn with abandon, and enabled one woman to discover how to move with the delicacy she'd always imagined but that her body continually undermined.

Fundamentally, this book is about reclaiming our naturally given capacity for sensation through sensing tactile motion – the sensation of motion through the interplay of muscles. Everything we are and everything we experience, including the quality of our experience, is affected by our musculature and the way we move, sit, stand, or walk.

Muscular misalignments are the patterned, narrowing, habit-forming paths to aches, recurring pain and eventual illness. It happens slowly, unconsciously, seemingly naturally, a silent behavioral virus. But the power that is contained in our muscular misalignments rests in how they are the quintessential unconscious psychic defense. And like all psychological defenses, they are a splitting-off from feelings. We are born with a sensate processing body before we ever form a cognitive self.

Following the techniques that I've developed over many years can give you a way to address damaging habits and divisions that have become ingrained and that remain mostly unnoticed. As your *attention from within the continuity of motion through the musculature* becomes established, you will begin to notice a subtle difference in your interactions with family, with friends, at work and throughout your life.

This *awareness from within* of ourselves in motion loosens the stiffened muscles of self-protection that developed unconsciously during the first few years of our lives. The practice of this awareness begins by coming alive to our feet's contact with the ground by sensing the contact of the sole of the feet with the ground. Our ability to consciously awaken to the simple sense of contact takes on life as a sensation that we can sense spreading through our feet and continuing upwards through the rest of our body.

Feelings arise naturally out of this tactile attention to the movement of motion throughout the body as constant. Though this movement is happening with everyone, the connection between muscles and feelings is not commonly made. But the connection can be acquired by anyone wanting to feel totally alive in the body. If you pay this sort of attention to the way you stand, move, and walk, any stiffness in your neck will loosen, your feet will touch the floor in a way that is grounding, your ankles will strengthen, and your lower back will become more aligned. And this will cause you to feel more connected and aligned on the inside.

INTRODUCTION

Although the teachings in this book are relatively easy to understand and implement, they took me more than forty years to fully understand. As a movement teacher, I became extremely conscious of the problems that children and adults had with their musculature and movement. Adults, especially, are generally not even aware that they're out of alignment or not in harmony. There is a disconnect between what they see and understand and what their muscles are doing that escapes their awareness. My effort to understand this disconnect led me to become a psychoanalyst. And that unusual combination of teaching movement techniques in conjunction with what I'd learned as a psychoanalyst led to this book.

This book is about reclaiming nature's evolutionary, God-given capacity for sensation. We can become alive to our feet's contact with the ground, to our balance, to our sense of presence. All of the complicated mind issues begin to dissipate by sticking to the sensation of contact as motion through the musculature.

Muscular misalignments are the way fear and repressions happen, blocking our spirit, closing off feelings, diminishing our energy, freezing the motion of love and understanding. The how and why of misalignments is the silent language which this book makes clear. Practical incremental adjustments can be made that evaporate patterns of pain and habits of denial, awakening that part of us that travels through our muscles: a smile, a sigh, a tear, laughter, our soul – to re-acknowledge the ground, the earth from which it arose.

Through my journey as choreographer, dancer, actor, director, and psychoanalyst – and primarily as a creative movement teacher – I've found a way for feelings to rise through attention to motion through the muscles. There is nothing to lose by trying. Attention to sensation is how it starts and how it continues.

CHAPTER 1

BELIEVING IN HOPE

My Father and Hope

> *Fear cannot be without hope nor hope without fear.*
> ~ Baruch Spinoza, Ethics

I flew in from New York to Detroit to see my sister and visit my dad at the nursing home. I sat to the right of my 87year-old father, who refused dentures because the adjustments were uncomfortable, refused hearing aids because during the test he experienced a shriek that was jarring, and was resolute about refusing the removal of his cataract as just another invasion on his sensations. Physical sensations of pain were too close to the emotional fears he managed to defend against.

It is only in the last few years, as I have reached 84, that I have come to grasp how profoundly sensations play a role in our thinking, values, and judgments and that considerations about how sensations affected my father so deeply have taken on some emotional clarity for me.

We sat to have afternoon tea and cookies on a bench at the table. Neither of us spoke. Perhaps we had arrived at a point in our relationship where words created a dissonance that neither of us wanted. He suddenly turned his head toward me and said, *"You have to have hope."* After six years at the nursing home, wheelchair bound, this unsolicited comment from him was both amazing and disturbing.

I don't know about him, but my dissonance immediately kicked in. I was shocked by his use of hope. I could hear the tension of disbelief in my voice. *"You gave up exercising to get stronger years ago,"* implying, you're not thinking straight. I was unusually disturbed. *"What is wrong with me? He is 87, just talking. Why are you giving him a hard time?"* Shame rattled my chest.

I felt ashamed by my dismissive put-down tone, as my questions tumbled out, I realized that I was demanding a coherence that had more to do with me than him. He always maintained a self-protective distance from being engulfed by demands, especially by his wife's fears, my mother whose need for security he could neither deal with nor appease. Fears and terrors, I've also come to recognize, have influenced my work and my life quite deeply.

His eyes narrowed in a way that has always said to me, *"You don't get it, do you?"* Then without missing a beat he reinforced his comment, *"You always know what happened yesterday, but you never know what will happen tomorrow."*

I thought his pronouncement simplistic, although it is true that we do not know what will happen tomorrow. What I didn't register was that he still found each day, a tomorrow, awaiting his interest. I wish I had been able to appreciate his curiosity. I heard *"You have to have hope,"* as a fantasy, a wish to dampen his disturbing feelings of the present.

Yet, something else resonated within me on a feeling level that I can best describe metaphorically as rain falling on a parched heart. A parched heart I didn't even know I had. I was sensing an internal vibration that speaks truth to us; it is physical, sensory, and spiritual. I still sense the vibrations just writing these words.

His abiding sense of curiosity, *"You don't know what will happen tomorrow."* has visited me many times over the years. How right he was. We don't know what will happen tomorrow; curiosity has a way of balancing our fearful mind. Curiosity intrigues our courage to try things out, to discover unanticipated pleasures, to discover truths we didn't know await us.

This book is about honoring my father, whose sense of hope has helped me through some awfully rocky passages in my life. I've come to honor how much of my movement work is a tribute to him, a way of understanding him psychologically through my movement exploration, a lifetime research project. I'm memorializing the integrity of his soul, and in turn, my own.

This book is not just about how to deal with the dismissal of sensations and how to keep the fantasies of curiosity alive. It is about the truth and power of our fearful mind and how by literally contacting the ground, we begin the retrieval of sensation, the reawakening of our body and soul to come alive.

We need to pay attention from within the body and there is a way to do this, *a simple, everyday way.*

Sensation Leads to Hope

> *We live on the leash of our senses.*
> ~ Diane Ackerman

> *..., so I settled into the deadness.*
> ~ Elizabeth

Considering *coming alive through sensations* brings to mind Elizabeth and Nina. Both of these women experienced *sensation* they hadn't felt for years.

Elizabeth, a psychoanalyst in her sixties, came to her very first class. I knew her as a senior analyst with a strong ballet background during her early youth. She had received a mailing from me and brought another analyst along with her from a dance class at the 92nd Street Y.

By the time she arrived I had already settled on the importance of the *4th toe line on the sole of the feet,* a line that runs from the middle of the heel to the 4th toe, the one next to the little toe. I'll describe at length the history and value of 4th toe line in a later section.

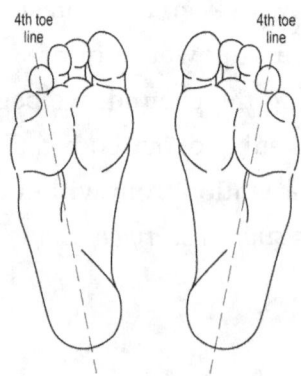

I remember Elizabeth standing just to my right facing me. Her eyes attentive, but her face solemn with a serenity, somewhat mysterious, that doesn't convey emotions easily.

I start the class by asking everyone to stand over the *4th toe line of the feet*. We all take a moment just to sense this initial instruction, requiring most often bringing the legs in closer to the center of the body.

"Oh, my god, I can feel my toe!" Elizabeth suddenly screamed. We were all shocked by her explosive scream. *"It went dead as a result of the medications I was taking during my late pregnancy. This is unbelievable!"* She was gasping with excitement. She couldn't stop herself, *"I talked to my obstetrician, saw a neurologist in an effort to deal with the toe gone dead, but no one knew what to do, so I settled into the deadness."*

We all turned towards her when she screamed and were dumbfounded by what she was telling us. No one had ever reacted to standing over the 4th toe line in the way that Elizabeth had. What came tumbling out in the throes of her discovery of sensation in a toe she hadn't sensed for so many years was totally captivating for all of us. All of the adults in this class were seasoned professionals with children, aware of the hazards of pregnancy, but, apparently, none of us had ever heard anything like this.

I was glad for her, but that standing over the 4th toe line could make a dead toe come alive. It had never occurred to me! After everyone shared their congratulations with her, the class resumed standing over the 4th toe line with a new sense of wonder.

The second story is about Nina, another psychoanalyst, who, along with her practice, writes about dance for a popular psychological magazine. She came to my attention via another psychoanalyst in class who read a review Nina had written about a choreographer she had seen at the Joyce theater. My student thought I would find it interesting and forwarded it to me.

I responded to the review, excited by the language and the emotional parallels that touched on the issues I've come to consider important about dance and movement training. I quickly dashed off a letter of praise, with a short note about my work along with a copy of my book, *The Way of the 4th Toe: Into the Feeling Body*. Happily, she e-mailed within a few days, and we set up a lunch to meet and talk.

When we met, before the first sip of wine, she told me, *"Jack, both my third and fourth toes, on both feet, that have been dead for years unbelievably came alive as I tried out what you described at the very beginning of the book. I was amazed!"*

Once again, I was shocked by this reference to toes coming alive. Admittedly, it was a number of years since Elizabeth first burst out in class about her toe returning from the dead. With Nina, I was taken aback by the event of her four toes coming alive, two on each foot. And this, coming from a woman who was a dance lover, aware and sensitive to her physical experience, added to my wonder and speculations.

When I discovered the value of how arches naturally arch, promoting muscular alignment by standing over the *4th toe line*, the notion that this could make "dead" toes come alive was not even a faint possibility in my mind. All of my specific instructions were aimed at fostering a more physically sensed improvisational dance.

Standing over the 4th line on the sole of the feet begins to realign the 40 muscles and 27 bones in the foot. Fortunately, both Elizabeth and Nina already had enough flexibility that simply bringing their attention to this specific alignment resulted in what they experienced as miraculous.

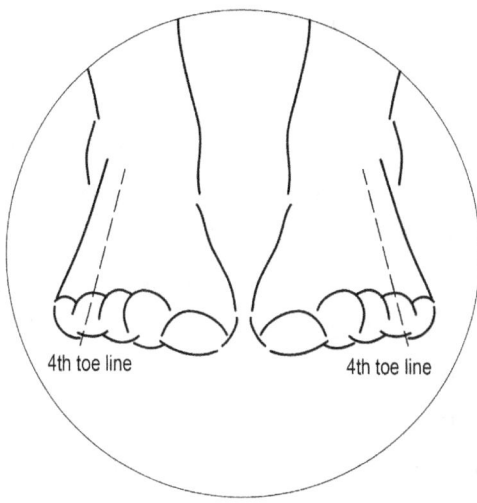

(If you try it, change only as much as you can without forcing. The changes will happen each time you try it.)

Reawakening *sensations* is the *phoenix rising from the ashes*. This Greek mythological tale[1] is perfect symbolically, in that the phoenix is reborn from its dead corpse, just as their toes arose from deadness.

What is it about *sensations* that speaks so loudly to us? *Sensations* tell us what is hard or soft, what is bright or dark, what is loud or inaudible, what smells sweet or musky, what is bitter or salty, when we're hungry or bloated, when there is pain, but they also trigger memories, judgments, and feelings and these accompany each and every sensory experience. We know which sensations are fun, which we hate, which excite

---

1 Book of Mythological Creatures, Friedrich Johann Justin Bertuch

us, and which bore us to tears. Sensations are incredibly rich in emotional meaning. If a sensation connected to an emotional experience is too painful, we may deaden the sensation. The internal musculature tightens automatically, a natural reaction to pain, which the developing mind remembers as the right thing to do. But this all happens quite unconsciously, way before we discover it and do it on a more conscious level. Some people even relish with pride their capacity for pain. We deaden and believe that we have buried the feelings associated with it or transformed it into its opposite – excitement.

My father avoided sensations that were or could be painful. I came to understand that it was his physical way of deadening the feelings of anger, which were so painful in their implications. He never spoke about those feelings or the circumstances around those feelings. Living, surviving, making a living, having a little fun, plus a little politics – all of this pretty much consumed his life. He was not a complainer, and he had a delightful sense of humor. I suspect we all have our own favorite ways for doing the same thing. We all avoid many sensations. We all do.

I recently heard one patient sheepishly reveal moments when he did not know what was real, the inside or the outside as if the issue is belief, rather than the feelings, he didn't know where to put the feelings – *"Is it me or is it what is happening to me?"* Of course, they are almost always both.

There is no feeling without sensation or sensation without feeling. You can intellectually separate the physical from the spiritual, which may evoke a sensation of peacefulness, as if sensations have stopped asking for attention. But they are twins living together side by side unless something awful happens that tears them apart. When that happens, we end up living split-off lives, arguing about reality, out of touch with a lot of sensations, out of sync with our feelings.

When awareness comes into our sensations, whatever we are experiencing comes alive, both the good and the bad. Feelings begin to flow, time disappears, and hope is raised in our hearts.

I wish I could have spoken with my dad about this.

Circulation Is Health and Hope

Elizabeth and Nina's toes came alive because the arteries that feed into the tendons open up to the river of life – *circulation*. Circulation is the blood supply to all body tissue, providing oxygen and nutrients to the cells and carrying carbon dioxide and waste products away.

There is no question in my mind that Elizabeth and Nina's sense of revelation was the consequence of circulation feeding the nerves, opened by the rearrangement of muscles over the 4th toe line. It is a little more complicated than this, but it's their muscular interaction that made sensation come alive to their consciousness.

Let me cite a rather dramatic example: *I looked at his aging, bony feet aghast at the dirt between his toes. It didn't fit with this intelligent, sophisticated professorial man. As I continued to teach, my eyes wandered over to his feet again to realize that it wasn't a lack of cleanliness, it was a lack of circulation. Over the course of a few months, or maybe it was longer, since it wasn't the central focus of my teaching, the blackness disappeared. The change was so significant to him, he became a committed student for many years.*

A primary physiologic function of muscles is to stimulate arteries to pump blood through the body and back to the heart. A primary psychological function of muscles is to protect against disturbing sensations. We stiffen muscles against fear. Muscles contract rhythmically to let us know we're hungry. Muscles make the blood throb in excitement. The brain talks to organs through muscles. Sagging muscles weaken the pulse of circulation, and overly tight muscles narrow the flow of circulation. We need activity for health.

Exercise works muscles. Bad exercises *misalign* muscles, which affects circulation, contributing to eventual injury and abetting disease, which you may not be aware of immediately. But ask dancers or football players about the price they pay for their dreams. Placing our body over the 4th toe line of the sole of the foot can dramatically stimulate blood flow. Imagine, how incredible it is that 40 muscles and 27 bones can rearrange with each other for blood to flow more easily so that nerves can be fed, allowing for sensations to be perceived by our mind. Skin darkness disappears, and dead toes come alive. Sensing the 4th toe line in our feet is specific, which is why I used to begin classes with this directive. I cannot stress enough that blood is a boulevard, the Champs-Elysees of the body, delivering food to the cells and transporting waste away.

Sheila, a woman in her fifties, like many older students do, immediately let me know that she has had problems with her lower back. Given my way of approaching these issues, I told her, "The minute you sense a stress on your lower back, stop, and let me know, so I can give you a, hopefully, helpful suggestion." Because she is a person who likes to keep going, she seldom followed this advice. Continuity meant more to her than what she was sensing. I took the opportunity to mention a general principle

I've followed since the seventies, namely, "the antidote to pressure (tension) is weight. *The very second you drop the weight of holding up, the muscles relax, stretch, bringing the support of the body closer to the floor, and the tension begins to dissolve." She began to flex her knees more when bending the torso and to stretch the back of the legs, and her back worries began to dissipate.* Every time we follow this general principle, the muscles open up and circulation is automatically promoted.

Circulation is the reason why nurses are instructed to get you out of bed after an operation as soon as possible. Doctors advise exercise along with medications. Circulation affects us on the most concrete levels. Every psychological defense, be it denial, disavowal, regression, acting out, splitting, et al., creates muscular tension, an instinctive physical defense against feelings that are threatening to our identity, affecting the body's flowing biochemical resistance to fight off viruses floating in the air. It is always a matter of circulation.

My father's stroke, I strongly suspected, was the consequence of his repression of feelings going back to age seven, when, since his father was gone, he was pulled out of school to help his mother in the open-air market, to sleep there and guard the sacks of grain. This was one of an incredibly few stories that I wove together from what he shared about growing up. His constant physical laboring work probably kept his circulation going for a long time, but the constant constriction of muscles eventually narrowed the flow to such an extent that a stroke became an eventuality.

The expression *bad blood* comes to mind. Like so many idioms expressive of what we all understand about the body that has been passed on from generation to generation as folk wisdom.

Exercising with a relaxed body, with flexed knees, and with a constant sense of the floor is our best defense against unwittingly creating more problems as we exercise. Understanding and practicing the "how" and "why" of the 4th toe placement will *realign* the flow of blood between muscles, allowing nerves to register sensations.

My father's philosophic, psychological sense of hope became increasingly more real for me as I discovered through my teaching the simple ways that hope rises like flowers to the sun's rays, as circulation opens the musculature's sensory awakening.

Choice is an Option, NOT the Solution

Hope is a good feeling. When feeling holds a promise, like a wish. Hope is the partner wish needs.

Circulation and sensations are not a wish. They are working all the time without our having to think about them. If circulation isn't working health is at stake. If sensation isn't working, there is either a neurologic problem or incredible psychological denial at work. In either case our survival is in danger. What we don't sense, need to think about, becomes potentially serious.

Muscles pump circulation and react to sensations. It all works seamlessly like a trinity. We didn't have to think about the swallowing muscles or breathing muscles. Fingers moved, head lifted, we turned in the crib, sat up, and stood because muscles were consciously working. We didn't choose to accomplish these activities; they happened.

Unless terror traumatically froze our movement, or some person sadistically controlled our movement, made us feel deeply afraid, these naturally evolving accomplishments slowly begin to register as our "Will." Will is a power that becomes noticeably assertive by age two and unmistakable at four. We know these ages as the negative twos and the negative fours. Will, is strength. Stop for a second and check out the sensation of your body as you think about Will, notice a tightening internal sensation, a sense of determination, muscles preparing to fire. Will and intention are inseparable

Muscles fire with desire, they become agents of the mind. We train muscles to fulfill wished for skills. Muscles as agents of the mind fulfill the wishes we envision for the future.

The fact is that we cannot move without muscles. Muscles move bones. It is through muscles that actions are realized. Muscles are the present, they are the "now." But we don't experience them in the present because they belong to the future, to our aims, our intentions, our hope. They belong to the mind.

Lorna, a student, twisted her ankle dancing at a family party. Her torn tendons required an operation and a long period of physical therapy. She described it as "an accident of high heels." When she returned to class all she could think about was the memory of pain.

The high heels compromised her sense of support. Unconsciously, her pleasure dancing belonged to her mind because all of her energy lifted upwards toward her chest, shoulders, face, and neck. Hers was a lifetime of misalignments in the muscles of her feet, through her ankle and into her calves, unconsciously compensated for with the contracted musculature of her buttock and lower back. All of these unrecognized misalignments and compensations registered emotionally in her mind as due to feeling "high," to letting go. She blamed her pleasure as if that was the issue. Given that she came out of a conservative household, her moral background was reinforced. The understanding that she lost a sense of her muscles in the present was nowhere in her sights.

Patterned muscular misalignments never came up between her and her doctor or physical therapist. My way of talking about the connection between alignment and feelings, of being in the present is not a part of their medical training.

Since, our alignment or misalignment develops without our awareness, we commonly don't give it a second thought. When either is brought to our attention, the tendency is to fall back on habit, genetics, or remembered physical accidents that might have impacted alignment. The impact of emotional development, of likes and dislikes are seldom considered as profoundly affecting the way that muscles work. Whatever it is we tried either worked to our satisfaction or was rejected because it didn't. That is more or less the way it works. Right?

Choosing what we enjoy or rejecting what we don't is a freedom we defend, but it doesn't address the physical problems that led to the choice we defend. *Choice is an option not a solution.*

Avoiding pain muffled Lorna's wish for the pleasure of dance. Rebuilding trust in her body to overcome her fear of a permanent impairment took time. The residue of fear even after pain has been dealt with never quite leaves us. It appears to have a permanent home in our minds. *It leaves only as we deal with the specifics of what resulted in pain. Only then does the fear dissolve.* Working on her misalignments to sense her contact with the floor, to sense motion through the muscles of her feet, to sense the support of her ankles, all of this was difficult, because she had to let go of fun as the problem. Her moralistic attitude of restraint, coming out of a religious constrictive household, lived in contrast to her wish for freedom. Both of them needed to be recalibrated to make room for a sensitivity to muscular sensation. Only then could her fear evaporate. Only then could she begin to experience mind and body as one.

Pleasure engages our whole self, body and mind. Pain splits the body from the mind that only wants to get rid of it.

The Eureka experiences for Elizabeth and Nina were toes coming alive. What they had lived and thought of as dead rose to live again. Becoming alive within sensations of what were deadened parts and aspects of ourselves, becoming alive to forgotten experiences, surprises us, as more of our body and perceptions are working.

Neither Elizabeth nor Nina, nor Lorna were thinking about hope. Hope happens when what was in deadness is reborn out of the ashes of disregard. When the musculature opens, our spirit emerges.

Sensing the muscular alignment is different than sensing the outside, seeing what is outside or hearing what is outside or smelling what is outside or tasting what is outside.

My father made choices, some conscious, most, from my present perspective, unconscious. His choices fostered his sense of independence that unfortunately left out his body, the part through which his choices became a reality. He left out the solution aspect of choice.

Rekindling our sensory awareness of motion through muscles is a choice and a solution.

CHAPTER 2

HOW HOPE IS LOST

Movement, Mind, Feelings

> *Keep me as the apple of the eye;*
> *hide me under the shadow of thy wings....*
> **~ Psalms XVII, 8**

Commonly, we move with a goal in mind. We get out of bed to wash and dress. We walk to the kitchen to make coffee. We stand up in order to get somewhere. We lie down to rest. There is almost always a reason determining what we are doing with our body.

Paying attention to motion through the muscles as we fulfill the tasks of the day would seem beside the point if it ever even occurred to us. Goals, aims, intentions orient us mentally, but can leave our bodies behind, even though we seem to be here physically.

Aim oriented actions use the body as a tool for their fulfillment and our apparent gratification. This is one of the three personality perspectives I described in how people experience their body in my book, *The Way of the 4th Toe: Into the Feeling Body.*

Using my body as a tool was my basic perspective throughout most of my life. It is how I tried out for the track team at Cass Tech High in Detroit on a cork track above the gym floor, so small that running a mile involved an incredible number of turns around the oblong track. The person assigned to set the pace had won the Michigan State cross-country meet the year before. I stayed with the first mile pace easily, then suddenly collapsed, into one of the track's wooded corners, muscles throbbing in exhaustion, heart pounding uncontrollably. I had absolutely no sense I was becoming exhausted until I collapsed. In retrospect, I was completely disconnected from my sensations. There was my mind-driven aim, and then my reliable body ready to do what I wanted… until it couldn't. My aim was never in question.

I continued on my quest to make the track team by trying high jumping, followed by pole-vaulting thinking I could do that. I functioned with a physical confidence demanding mastery at whatever I wanted to do. Whether the body is working in an integrated way was immaterial, as long as it didn't get in the way of my aim, in the way of my doing what I was trying to do and my being great at it.

But when the musculature is not working together, it is implicitly disconnected, meaning that the effort inherent in an activity is not suspended throughout the body in feeling. The illusion or delusion that our body is together is based on the certainty of our intention, our wish and fantasy. But, as T.S. Eliot says in *The Hollow Men*:

> "Between the idea
> And the reality

> *Between the act*
> *And the motion*
> *Falls the Shadow."*

There is a difference between thinking or visualizing the unity of the body in motion and sensing from within our togetherness of motion through the musculature. My body belonged, in an important sense, exclusively to the primitive *omnipotence* of my psychological development—a normal unconscious fantasy connection that every infant has to the mother's power, who in the child's imagination is unquestionably capable of doing anything, i.e., everything to keep us alive, comfortable, and safe. This maternal (or caregiver's) presence is a fundamental source of trust. If you had 'good enough' care and developed this trust, it helps to deal with all sorts of problems in life. If you weren't fortunate enough to acquire that trust, fear and worry follows every step of the way. This trust deficit is something we can, with a concerted effort, get over, but it is not easy.

A case in point: Max came to see me for a private session. *"My knees feel weak when I walk up to the lectern to give my weekly sermon."* He delivered his weekly sermon at a high-security prison in New York State; the sermon was a part of his practicum as a doctoral student at a Theological Seminary. *"My psychoanalytic sessions haven't managed to affect my experience,"* he told me. He readily acknowledged the fear of walking down the aisle past a room full of high security convicts. *"I can't stop my knees from buckling."*

Max had a muscular body. There was nothing spindly about it or in the way he spoke. There was, to all appearances, nothing spindly about him. *"Can you help me,"* he humbly asked?

I told him to *"Just walk around the studio,"* and noticed that his torso was lifted. He was top-heavy. *"Would you try dropping your torso down towards the floor, little by little, until you feel totally solid?"* Uncertain of my direction because he was double guessing me, trying to ascertain my motive, which was a fool's errand, because he was so out of touch with the psychophysical understanding I had begun to put together.

He continued lowering his torso, his knees bending more and more, until he ended up using his fisted hands on the floor like an ape. I continually encouraged him to keep bending until his knees stopped shaking. Then, quietly, and clearly surprised, he said, "The weakness is gone." He smiled.

The physical experience of lowering his body to such an extent got rid of his buckling knees, which he had attributed to an unconscious psychological fear. He was frustrated by not being able to control his fear with his mind. Coming to see me was an act of desperation. He was shocked by such a direct physical process eliminating the physical symptom he was certain was emotional. I suspect that the convicts coming for his religious sermon were not scary at all. His fear was what we term a psychosomatic symptomology, not based on what was going on around him but rather on an unconscious feeling that was being defended by his shaking knees, effectively diverting his attention from what he might be feeling.

He was psychologically knowledgeable enough to suspect his fear was visible to the convicts, an impression he didn't want to convey and that would impact negatively on his uplifting educative sermon. But he couldn't control what was happening to him. He, like so many of us, believed that our rational mind can zap fear away. The notion that getting in touch, as minimally as he did, with his body also affected his unconscious feelings was not a connection he had yet made.

"*Great. I'd like you to continue walking around the studio, lifting your torso very, very slowly so as not to lose the solidity you are sensing.*" As he followed this directive, his relaxed face and slight smile said it all.

I explained what had happened physically. "*Lowering your torso relaxed the musculature and the stiffness of the way you hold your spine. The musculature around the spine tightens when fear borders on terror. Your buckling knees were telling you that your fear was deeper than the way you were holding yourself together. Walking like an ape is your animal self, perhaps a more aggressive, tougher self than how you think of yourself. Your body was reacting to a part of yourself that is ashamed of fear, a fear you have yet to genuinely acknowledge. The lowering of your spine and the use of your fists to stabilize your balance affected a deeper part of yourself. You simply have to make room for that powerful aspect of yourself.*"

I left it at that without venturing any further into possibly deeper personal feelings.

I cite this case because it is a pretty good example of emotional aspects of self that are dissociated from our body, the sort of dissociation that makes our musculature work in a disconnected way, physically misaligned and emotionally out of sync.

Considering that he was scholarly and educated and in psychoanalysis, I assumed that he knew all about the Freudian theory of aggression and sexuality postulated as fundamental human drives. His intellect suspected, but his body hid his true, more private feelings.

I learned years later that he became a rather important person in his field, suggesting that he got in touch with his aggressive self and maybe his sexuality in a manageable way. His buckling knees made his dissociated unconscious real.

Satisfied with one more thing he could effectively control, he left, never to return. When I met him years later at a professional setting, he had no memory of our encounter, or possibly no memory of the transformative experience of his trauma.

Was leaving after one session the hubris of knowing without working it through the body? Or, did he learn all that he could understand from our little exploration that didn't meet with his grander view of emotional integration? Your guess is as good as mine.

Muscular misalignments are the quintessential unconscious psychic defense. Like all psychological defenses, they are a splitting-off from feelings. We are born with a sensate processing body before we ever form a cognitive self.

This unconscious separation from a process that precedes control becomes ever stronger as conscious thinking and choices become more central to our experience. Real solutions require a commitment to the inseparability of body and feelings or suffering a trauma that forces us to acknowledge the inseparability.

The body is the battleground of the unintegrated self.

Dissociations, Fixations, the Senses

Olivia had a piece of metal put into her ankle to repair a break resulting from an accident. Months of physical therapy, and repeated assurances from the surgeon that she was totally healed, could not dislodge her sensation, "I can feel the metal. I can't get over this cold, stiff object inside." She was fixated.

She appeared deeply troubled, conveying that she didn't expect it to change. As a psychoanalyst, I suspected that she was referring to something more personal, more buried than the metal in her ankle. But she already had a therapist,

Nothing moves when the mind fixates.

Her imagined sensation, imagined coldness, imagined stiffness, were sensations the doctor could not remove, and the physical therapists could note dislodge. But they felt totally real to her. No amount of assurance could convince her otherwise. And her self-recriminations were not helping to get rid of the cane she walked around with. The persistent sense of fear and her accompanying anger encased her mind and spirit as she was shrouded in this fixation.

She brought her boyfriend to the first session – expecting what? Was she imagining that I would abuse her spirit? She was afraid. After greeting him, I asked that he wait outside, while I talk to her. We began by sitting. I made sure to keep my chair sufficiently distant from her not to arouse a sense of invasion that her words *"I can't get over this cold, stiff object inside,"* suggested she was suffering from. I didn't want to tax her tolerance and the distrust by bringing her boyfriend suggested. Was she unwittingly revealing a persistent sexual fantasy, something inside that is *stiff and she can't get rid of it?* She was clearly talking about this piece of metal, but could this be a reference to something else? Such suppositions were plausible. But one is never sure of suppositions. You have to wait for evidence, for corroboration, for other comments that could give the notion some credence. Given the boundaries of the physical work, there might never be the opportunity for this.

I understood that the persistence of her discomfort meant that the motion of movement does not pass smoothly through her ankle and foot. I asked her to sit forward on the chair so that she would sense her heels on the floor without a doubt. Her legs were too close to each other so that the sensation on her heels fell mostly to their inside. I was verbalizing every observation, making sure that she understood that she wasn't just following directions because I was telling her what to do. We needed to be on the same page. The next step was chancy, *"Would you open your legs so the sensation over the heels falls on the middle of your heels?"* I sensed a critical moment in our transaction, noting that she might treat my suggestion as sexually invasive. She did move her legs. I looked down toward her heel conveying were my attention really was, in order to not reinforce her imagination. We proceeded incrementally, little by little, conveying that I would not force her to do anything that wasn't comfortable. Over a number of weeks of incremental changes, and eventually elementary rhythmic explorations, I watched the tension in her eyes relax.

She eventually gave up the cane in the studio, except when she walked outside on the street, maybe she wanted people passing by to make an accommodation for her condition. The cane eventually disappeared, as she reported, *"I have at times forgotten my limping and ankle all together."*

Following her wish that she would be able to dance at her wedding, I began to bring music into the sessions. After twenty sessions, she was able to move to the rhythm of the music. Her success in overcoming *the cold stiff metal* was physically based on changing her physical experience. The focus on reviving the sensations of her feet and the continuity of motion through her calves brought the actuality of motion to be more present than the memory of the metal and the associations that she imaginatively built up around something *cold inside of her*. The increasing facility of motion, as in Elizabeth and Nina's resurrection of sensation in their toes, was changing the coldness of repressed pleasure into the possibility of dancing at her wedding. The focus on the middle of the heels, of stepping over the middle of the heels, gave her a sense of control over the fantasies that enclosed her. The emotional success happened as the "pleasure" of movement increased, diminishing her reliance on *somaticizing the fear of pleasure* through her body.

Mark and The Time Machine

Every fixation diminishes the movement of the present

Mark, on the other hand, feels totally free despite a recurring lower back and hip problem, as he spins poetry, writes a novel about what preceded and what followed his fixation with death. He speculates rhythmically about the end game. He expresses himself with unchecked fluidity, a mind that pieces together thoughts, events as thoughts, feelings as thoughts, with the certainty of a time machine, simultaneously recording and translating. A time machine is a pretty good metaphor for a preoccupation with death.

The body tells a different story. Body pain is hard to dismiss. The nerves become inflamed and no matter how much healing fluid the body produces, the flame isn't easily extinguished.

We walked down the street and I asked if I could give him some suggestions that might work. He agreed. I put my arm around his shoulder as I spoke.

"Is it your right hip?"
"Yes."

"Would you move the right leg in closer to the left leg. Do you sense a difference?"
"Yes."

"You understand that by moving the leg in, the transference of weight is moving more easily through the musculature affecting the braced area that triggers the nerve?"

He followed my directions to the letter.

"Let's take a shorter stride as we're walking to make the transference of weight a little smoother, shifting from one leg to the next."

He excitedly shouted out to his wife who was walking behind us with my wife, *"Jack just cured my hip!"*

I took my arm off his shoulder, allowing him to celebrate his relief unencumbered.

"You know," I added, *"you have to remember what you did. But the next time the adjustments you make will be slightly different. Try to stay alive to the sensation of motion, otherwise you will keep trying to celebrate the memory of relief."*

The body, again, is the battleground of disconnected feelings. The mind spins webs around the thought. The repression generates Olivia's exhausting and crippling fixation, hoping to be able to dance at her wedding, as well as Mark's speeding mind trying to outrun the pain of loss, the loss of loves by forming images, dreamscapes, symbols that disavow the endangering physical misalignments as he ages.

Fixations tighten the musculature, squeezing veins and arteries, reducing the warming blood to a trickle. The body chills. The pressure in the belly pushes the finger out of the dyke that was holding back a consuming rage with whomever, for whatever reason, love was supposed to come.

Rage is a difficult feeling to deal with, especially when we are infants, toddlers, and children. At an early stage of life, before we can thrash our body around, rage is so traumatically frightening that we freeze. Our reaction is more like catatonia, a frozen pantomimic shape, unmovable. As infants, the whole-body rattles, squeezing the diaphragm, forcing the vocal cords into punctuated screams, because it is autonomic and not in our control. Falling asleep automatically exhausted extremely early in life has to do with how deeply feelings threaten our being. Toddlers thrash the body about, legs kicking, arms swinging, emitting sustained screams in their desperation, being in unrelenting frustration about a pain they cannot disavow. They continue to whimper, sniffling to catch their breath. Children cry, turning silence into a sealed-off room of memory and resolve not to trust. Adults, either enlarge the room of distrust or incrementally help the child find their way back to the movement of exchange.

Every fixation, regardless of what it is on, be it dance, sex, family, business, sports, philosophy, et al., affects all of our senses, diminishing the movement of the present.

Time again

Working with a woman in her late nineties, I was concerned about her state of mind, *I stroked the top of her hand and told her, "This is now. What remains,"* as I lifted my fingers away *"is memory, the wish for the touch, the fantasy of its pleasure, or the anger of its loss – fixations lead to dissociations."* She had undergone a very good analysis earlier in her life and was very knowledgeable psychologically. I was speaking to a very educated woman celebrated for her years of imparting wisdom and challenging insights.

We normally function with feelings flowing as the senses continuously inform the present. Unfortunately, the present is much too often overridden by purpose, and invariably parceled into memories of pleasure or pain. If pain dominates, the senses get blocked, eyes and ears are reduced to radar looking for signals of pain; the musculature shrivels, lessening the aliveness of the skin, our largest sensory organ, and conversely, we compensate with memories of pleasure to offset the pain. We function with this whirlwind of intention and imagination in a state of generalized anxiety.

Fixations form the basis for mastery; for Olivia, her body, and for Mark, his mind. Fixations are always experienced as the bottom line and serve as a point of departure: in Olivia's case, for control of the body, and in Mark's case for creative displacements. *Control and displacements* are overvalued, as the feelings underlying the fixation are defended like a medieval citadel, rationalized by the mind's marching banner – choice.

Freud's psychoanalytic considerations began with an effort to make conscious the dynamics of fixating that blocked energy.

His goal was to lift the fixation. When his explanation of dammed energy proved therapeutically inadequate, the complexity of the fixing adhesion shifted to hypothesizing mental structures fighting for dominance, for governance: The wild, uncontrollable Id is mediated by an executive functioning Ego that is in turn dominated by the parental, social, cultural or idealizing Superego. The energy of the primitive Id is so demanding that the moral, idealizing Superego makes an alliance with the Id, undermining the balancing functions of the Ego This alliance often drives artistic creations. It can however also result in impulsive acts of rationalized sadism.[2] This sounds complicated. Transactional Analysis, formulated by Eric Berne,[3] describes it this way: the "child" governed by the "parent" must be made reasonable by the "adult," an easier social paradigm for the American mindset.

Fixation is essentially a form of attachment. The frightening feelings are kept under wraps by an earlier learned protective system of magically holding on to a source of irrefutable, magical belief – the iconic mother, the universal energy, the scent given off by the never-to-be-extinguished candle at the altar of one's chosen saint. It is based on a powerful psychophysical memory. Fixation is an iron curtain that nothing can pierce, defending feelings

---

[2] Sigmund Freud, Beyond the Pleasure Principle, James Strachey (editor) Norton Library

[3] Games People Play, Eric Berne, M.D., Ballantine Books

that are intolerable and can't be processed. It is as if the self would crumble without the fixation.

How do we free fixations without collapsing the link that keeps the person related, as all attachments do? It is not easy or simple.

Fixations reroute the continually working senses: eyes stare or scan for danger, ears attune to hurt, skin recoils with anticipated intrusion. Our senses and feelings that work together at birth are split off one from the other. An internal embrace found in our musculature must quiet the whole body, like a mother's embrace rocking the baby from side to side to quiet its discomfort.

Sensations never stop working. Paying attention through sensations increases the aliveness of whatever we are involved with. Sensation of motion going through the musculature becomes easier and easier as one keeps differentiating *sensing motion through* muscles *from actions with* muscles. There is no shortcut to doing this. It is forever a personal process, a willingness to pursue the sensitivity.

It took me many years to pay attention to the minute incremental physical adjustments, and the ensuing subjective emotional elements that in conjunction are true to our complexity as human beings. *I learned to walk carefully over the middle of the heels, almost instantaneously dropping the shoulders, releasing the pelvic tilt that opens the space for the diaphragm to move fully. I began to see the length of the street, feel the sun on my body, and the air on my skin.*

Awareness is Practical

Weak-kneed Max was stuck in his emotional experience of fear. Fear is the name his mind assigned to what he was feeling. This was not a conscious name, it is one of the feelings we are all born with, so we know it well. His buckling knees were only the physical reflection of what was inaccessible to his conscious mind. It's what we commonly call, *mind over matter*. What surprised him as a consequence of our work, was the shift of *what is over what*. The change of body posture eliminated the fear, altering *mind over matter, to body over mind*.

The shift reestablished a different and more primitive order of experience, rearranging his hierarchal thinking with *mind* as first, to *body* as first. Mind simply collects, registers, and eventually rearranges in all sorts of ways, from helpful or acceptable ways, to crazy ways.

Stomach information and brain are in constant communication. *Sensations* feed the brain. The brain responds to them by telling muscles to activate organs to release the chemicals to deal with the *sensation*. We eventually come to think of our brain as *mind* to control *sensation*. The common developmental process happens unconsciously and is consequently a source of our great confusion about *sensations* as controllable, by-passing the more complicated metabolic process. Admittedly, we not only want to control sensations of pain, but also sensations of excitement that we may experience as overwhelming or inappropriate. All controls of sensation involve some degree of bodily stiffening, dampening the nerves, constricting circulation. But what is most damaging is closing the gates of emotional awareness to what the sensation is letting us know. This process is the negative form of *mind over matter*.

Max registered how his body's muscular and postural changes altered the "shame" of a weak body with fear.

The *practical awareness* of the motion of muscles shifted his emotional fixation of fear and shame. I am sorry that he didn't continue to make that *practical awareness* a more readily available sensitivity.

Overcoming emotional fixations is based on becoming aware of dissociated *sensation* and dissolving the separation of awareness and sensation. It is tapping into the original fish-like quality of the fetus in utero.

Having said all this, you might rightly ask, "Why then do I have to develop an awareness about a sensitivity that is hardwired at my core, whether I am conscious of it or not?"

It's a good question.

The answer is simple. Aren't you glad to be able to pick up your fork, cut the meat on your plate, able to say *ouch* when something hurts, or *ah*, when it feels good? We come to appreciate experiences from which we've learned a lot. They have unconsciously and consciously shaped our personalities. The physical skills we've developed make us independent. The social skills make us adaptive. We value our survival skills.

These not remembered or recalled acquired skills shape our uniqueness. I can't conceive of any interest, artistic, managerial, scientific or even criminal which isn't a unique process of discernment. The quality of *Awareness* is the result of growing up, becoming smarter, and hopefully wiser.

Isn't this true of cooking, hunting, any business, election campaigns, therapy, surgery, dressing, basketball, and dancing? Is there any activity that doesn't improve through deepening awareness? Stress management requires awareness. *"Know thyself"* is a birth of awareness. Mediation is a freeing of awareness. Respecting another person's way of thinking and of feeling is a heightening of *awareness*. Intuition is an instant and comprehensive *awareness*. Impulses are a short-circuited physical form of *awareness*. Achieved awareness is not simply a mindful goal; it is the result of *practical* experience, of specifics, regardless of what kind of activity or skill is involved.

Sensing motion through muscles, from muscles to muscles is an awareness of **self-perception** *that is without doubt practical and tactilely specific, distinct from the aforementioned activities.*

Awareness is Specific

It is always specific, like the bricklaying of a fireplace or sending a telescope into the far reaches of the universe. The more specific one senses the actual motion through the muscles, the clearer the co-ordination of movement, the more encompassing the synergy of the action.

I am reminded of Shira. She appeared for classes after a hiatus of over thirty years. The young mother of three was now in her seventies. She still had that small petite body that floated back to mind. She quickly interrupted my memory of her younger self by alerting me about her arthritis, which had already resulted in a rotator cuff operation. She was totally healed but couldn't raise her arm above a certain point. Her fear was obvious. The tone of her voice was severe. Her pain was not to be dismissed.

"Do the same arm rotation exercise at a lower level that feels comfortable," was my "practical" suggestion and demonstration. Her desperation to feel better – and she had tried already in so many

different ways – made her do what I suggested very carefully. She was exhausted by pain. I asked her to apply this minimal effort to every exercise. Her arms were eventually able to lift and turn fully. She was able to heed my advice, and that, over time, made all the difference in the world. She began to dance much more freely.

Fear is not something to take lightly. The person has good reason to be afraid beyond whatever they are telling us, beyond what seems obvious.

Shira was able to enjoy the drama of her gestures, the release of motion and rhythmic control of impulses, like flashes of light, appearing and disappearing. The more profound fear showed up whenever she turned, as if the spin of the body would consume her like an unexpected whirlpool coming out of nowhere while sailing on calm waters.

Reaching this fear took much longer. Her watchful self-observing eye needed to be lowered into her feet and the ground. After all these years I am still amazed how long it takes for this to happen.

The slow cumulative impact of assimilating the interplay of muscles is now allowing her to breathe through the turns.

She thought that her only fear was the arthritis, but it went deeper. The specificity of work gave her a grounded and grounding security that allowed her to finally not somaticize her deeper mental demon, the blocks that quite a good psychoanalysis had not removed; the fear lifted for her, allowing her to turn in space.

The repression of feelings can be seen in the instantaneous tightening of muscles in specific parts of the body, cutting off the organic flow of motion. We wonder what suddenly happened, what made for the sudden tightening? Or as most often happens, it is not sensed at all. It just happens. We just happen.

I now think of physical disconnects as unconscious emotional dissociations. The repetition of gestures and forms is equally a cutting off of the organic flow of feelings, like a record stuck in a groove or jumping tracks.

You may have a very skilled sense of balance in how they release and contain physical impulses, or a seemingly seamless rhythmic continuity, but as you become accustomed to observing the continuity of motion flow through muscles you can detect the cutting off, the dissociations, the jolt of unconscious fear.

In the winter of 1958-59, when I attended Juilliard, the first cultural break in the Cold War between the U.S. and the U.S.S.R. was the import of the Bolshoi Ballet Co. by the famous impresario, Sol Hurok. The relatively small dance community of New York City was invited to a rehearsal at the old Metropolitan Opera House. All of us sat in the first ring balcony, that's how small our dance community was at the time. Short snippets of various ballets by principals and corps de ballet demonstrated the impressive dramatic character dancing of the company. The small interludes left no doubt about the skilled brilliance of the dancers. Finally, from the down stage right wing entered Galina Ulanova, the prima ballerina of the company. Dressed in gray tights, gray leotard, gray leg warmers, and a gray short-sleeved sweater. She passed another gray sweater that was draped over her shoulders to a young dancer. A folded kerchief bound her short curled hair.

Tchaikovsky's Swan Lake music came on as this diminutive woman danced and folded downward into the trembling throws of the dying swan. The smallest little movement of her hands consumed her whole body as I watched transfixed, not by a consummate ballerina's hands, but by death itself. Shivers ran down my spine looking at death happening before me. It was a transcendent experience seldom repeated throughout the years of watching dance, attending theater, and looking at art.

Ulanova's movement melded the physical intent with the emotional essence of the choreography. Technique and the dancer disappear, we experience empathically a truth that is a part of all of us. Dramatically stated, life and loss are essential and unavoidable for all of us.

The unique transcendent experience with Ulanova sustained endless hours of training, invigorated years of teaching discoveries, and remained an embodied feeling of my hope.

Transcendence bathes us in light. Living feelings make it personally real.

CHAPTER 3

LOST IN FEAR

The Magical Body of Denial

Her infant son was in surgery undergoing a complicated operation. Leanne, the mother, a celebrated intellectual, was shaking, feeling she would go out of her mind. A standard line from my teaching, **"Feel your feet on the ground,"** *popped into her head. She repeated it over and over, again and again, holding her mind through a grounded body. "Thinking of the ground saved me from going crazy," she later told me in gratitude.*

During the surgery, Leanne felt destroyed by her helplessness, her not being able to do anything for her son. The prospect of losing him was unendurable, she felt she wouldn't be able to survive it. She was bound inseparably to her son. The connections in our hearts with those we love become porous at moments like these. The extraordinary orienting power of the mind that we commonly take for granted can evaporate.

I am struck by my sudden recollection of my step-aunt, a survivor of the Holocaust, who, along with her fellow inmates escaped death in the forest, when allied planes flew overhead and the German soldiers lined up to shoot them scattered for cover. She stood at the graveside in Detroit as her mother's casket, made of pine in accord with orthodox Jewish law, was lowered. Crying uncontrollably, she suddenly began to move towards the grave, ready to jump onto the casket with cries of increasing pain. My father, her stepbrother, and my mother forcefully grabbed her at the edge of the grave, increasing her wild howls.

This graveside scene took place longer ago than I can remember. But it has never left me. No doubt, I too am bound beyond the boundaries of my mind. Like Max, Leanne was one of those highly calibrated, sensitive people who was able through her scholarship to have the illusion of putting whatever is happening in its proper place. Unable to *control* what was happening was driving her to a place where she wished, like the infant/toddler in all of us, that her thought could crack the translucent surface between reality and fantasy, between this world and the next.

As children, magical thinking underwrites our imagination: we believe that grabbing our teddy bear can stop the screaming of our parents, or we cross our fingers to make wishes come true. Even as adults, gamblers rub the dice to make the magical seven come up when they roll on the green felt, as if rolling their childhood selves on the grass. Magical thinking doesn't simply end. Outside of superstitions, our behavior is witness to our implicit belief in the causality of all sorts of thoughts and actions that have no causal connections in fact. Magical thinking can be dismissed as childish delusion, but it is a powerful reminder of the power of wishing, of our playing with the fringes of the garment of hope.

I walked out of the hotel in Paris, angry as hell, grabbing my writing pad in its black leather cover hoping to find a friendly corner café to pour out my anger. I walked around for a while to dissipate the tension in my throat and chest. A wandering tourist looking at my self-involvement assumed that I was Parisian and asked in English for directions. This momentarily startled me out of my fixation and my raging. It cooled me down. I continued to walk, stumbling across a jewelry store. I bought a silver necklace with an enameled tiny pouch that, when opened, released a chained little silver heart. I returned to the hotel and gave it to my wife. She has hardly ever taken it off. A magical gift. My anger wasn't resolved but my hope found an icon to represent my wish for her love.

In general, most of us outgrow this magical mindset, but traces remain throughout our life. Magical thinking can make fear disappear, transform rage into rap songs, and desire into a multitude of notes in a sonata.

It is not uncommon to try *not to think* about fear as a way to stop the terrorizing effect of our boundaries collapsing. Wishing, hoping, thinking, as a shield against the piercing arrows of terrorizing feelings stiffens the musculature against the shapeless devil – fear.

I suspect that most people readily understand that the greater the terror, the flimsier the sheathing around our soul, the stronger the denial. The inner voice says, *"I don't care about the past, it's long ago. I don't even remember."* The dismissive reaction is not uncommonly worded as, *"What repression are you talking about?"*

Blaming follows denial like the web spinning from the spider.

The musculature is a shield against feelings. The feelings remain hidden as long as the muscular tension is retained. The cause of the terror – impotence, abandonment, loneliness, attachment, desire – is masked. In the process, our openness and receptivity is buried.

The magical *body/mind* fantasies – our omnipotent bodes, and omniscient minds – are driven underground as we grow up; they are immersed in our day-to-day realities, work, shopping, answering emails, getting gas.

The energy of these omnipotent and omniscient fantasies is both exhilarating and terrifying. There is an endless list of substitutions that feel undeniably real. We parachute, bungee jump off bridges, whitewater raft down the Colorado river, go to war, or fall prey to addiction, try out serial sexual liaisons, become exquisitely controlled dancers, imagine we are saviors of the world…

The following is a more common example of the magical mindset within the context of an improvisation class.

Bonnie moves in an individual improvisation. I watch her moving into space, her back somewhat tense, her neck held awaiting an internal sensation that will initiate the continuity of her dance. The continuity begins with leaning into her right shoulder and arm circling the space as if creating barriers to fend off attacks. Her right shoulder and right elbow leaning into the center of the circle makes for a magical moment like a curtain about to be parted. Once this sequence starts, she is unaware of dancing in her magical mindset. Her attention to the specifics of motion through the muscles is drowned in her imagination of herself dancing.

Bonnie unlike Leanne and Max taps into the magical mind through a subjective body pattern of movement and spatial motion. This has gone on for many years. Although it has begun to change, her magical body still struggles with her newly found attention to the *interplay of muscles loop*.

Why don't we more readily recognize our disappearing act? What built-in system do we have that allows us to miss ourselves, to slip away from ourselves, lie to ourselves?

Our capacity for denial is an ingredient in our being.

"You didn't see it coming? She was controlling from the get-go."
"What can I tell you, I didn't see it?"

Denial is psychologically extraordinarily powerful. We are dismissive of the power of our infantile fantasy, negating thoughts and feelings as *"just plain crazy ideas,' '...never have thought..."* Mythologies have characters that can change forms, alter reality by their thoughts, gods that are not to be fooled with; we find the same sorts of magical powers and transformations in some of our Sci-Fi and horror movies. These are tied to the ways that as toddlers we experienced our environment as vast and incomprehensible, and the times we were subject to the outbursts of an out-of-control parent. We are also struck daily by news stories of people that have fallen prey to their fantasies of power and the havoc that they cause.

What happens on a physical level when denial is at work? Just recently I listened to a tragic story of denial.

Diana, while away giving a lecture, heard by phone from her overweight sister that her mother had lost twenty pounds in a month. "Isn't that great, she wanted to lose weight," her sister said. Diana was stunned. *Mom is gravely ill,* she thought. She rushed home. When she asked her mother if she was okay, her mother responded, "Oh, sweetie, I'm OK: really, perfectly fine. You worry about me too much." Within a relatively short time her mother died of cancer in her arms.

Denial is the defense of choice for addicts. Denial shows up in the most unexpected ways in the body. Fear tenses muscles. Terror tenses tendons. Anyone who has experienced fear knows this. Denial makes it difficult to sense the *motion of movement* through the elasticity of muscles.

Melody, small-boned, in a tight narrow body, can't tolerate knee or sitting exercises. Corrections come and go like the wind whistling through the trees. She deeply appreciates my ideas about the body but has a lot of trouble sensing the elasticity of muscles bending or straightening. The interplay of muscles is a concept for her, not an experience. Paradoxically, her improvisational patterns, bordering on the bizarre, both as patterns and in the dynamics of their progression, are becoming more pliant. They are smoother now than when she started classes.

She had this magical way of taking in what she sees; it kept her dependent on others. But she refused to acknowledge the process through which this was happening. Acknowledging this it would make her independent.

She is adamantly individualistic but denies separateness by not relating to the elasticity of the muscles through which movement **must** happen. Her relationship to the body remains *the magical body of denial.*

Denial Reversed

The disturbing omnipotent and omniscient fantasies that surround us as infants – *brilliant auras of light enveloping us like magic spheres. Eyes we are too afraid to look into, like Medusa's.*[4] *Moses' face so bright after returning from his second trip to the mountain with the ten commandments, that he needed to wear a veil to speak to the people.*[5] These are all mystical visions. As toddlers–*monsters pass through windows, through impermeable surfaces like ghosts, spirits with or without physical bodies.* For children *bright red hair could be a sign of secret powers.* "*I used to feel when I jumped that I could stay up in the air forever,*" a former professional dancer once told me. All of these magical mental sensory experiences slowly get put aside, as we learn to dot our i's and cross our t's. These mythic experiences, so real when we are young can be *reversed* by the very same mind that trembled in fear and wonder. "*I can't*" can be transformed into "*I can.*" Obama used reversal to great effect.

Reversals can change fate into an opportunity for choices. Choices liberate us from the limitations of infancy. The mind in the process of making choices becomes increasingly more confident, dominant, proud, and, too often, arrogant and dismissive of what we feel. It happens, incrementally, without warnings, sealing us off from the sensory world of feeling.

The sensory mind that freezes in the threat of "obedience, or else..." Can reverse through its opposite, movement.

Walking away from the sandbox, toddlers stop in fear as their mother calls out their name, once, twice, and then, they *reverse* their obedience by continuing to walk away, using movement as their song of separation, of independence. You can see this happening at any sandbox in any playground.

---

4   A beautiful Greek woman turned into a monster, anyone who looked into her eyes was immediately turned to stone.

5   Old Testament, Exodus 34:29-35

Movement is the Archenemy of Terror

Bailah, eighty-five, just shy of five feet tall, had suffered a major stroke that had left her right-side limp. She was referred by a psychoanalytic colleague, who shared with me that as a young woman, Bailah loved dance class, and thought that working with me might help her recovery.

With her analyst and accompanied by an aid, Bailah settled on the floor, although I had set up two chairs for us. The analyst and I spoke for a bit, although I kept looking over at Bailah.

I asked them to leave while I worked with Bailah alone. She sat and collapsed inwardly, like an infant, legs opened, displaying the oversized diaper she was wearing. As I approached her, I had a self-conscious sense of her sizing me up with eyes lifted from a dropped face, thinking, "What is this young whippersnapper going to do for me?" I was in my late sixties at the time. The effects of her having suffered a stroke were unmistakable; it had left her right side incredibly limp. She took my outstretched hands as I helped her to stand. She was strong enough to use my strength to stand herself up. We stepped over to the two chairs. She lost her balance on every third step. I stopped each time, before going on. Looking me straight in the eyes, she said, "Your hands are cold. You must have a warm heart." I don't really know what made her decide to connect with me. Was it my outstretched fingers helping her to rise? Was it how I was stopping for her to regain balance? Was it my voice? She sensed my touch, and it felt cold to her. Did she figure out that I was slightly apprehensive, or was the coldness her lack of circulation? She quickly added, "You must have a warm heart!" I sensed seduction in her smile. "Thank you," I responded, as if what she said was a straightforward compliment. She repeated, "cold hands, warm heart" a number of times, confirming the pre-Alzheimer diagnosis she had been given at the hospital that my colleague had also shared with me.

I proceeded cautiously to test whatever strength she could muster on her right side, assessing the amount of voluntary movement available. I continually praised her efforts by sharing my surprise over how much she was able to do. I tested her ability to lift a bent right leg to strengthen her quadriceps, and then extend the rest of her leg. We did this again and again to strengthen the psoas muscle reaching into her lower back. The psoas is essential for practically any movement. We did the same for the other leg. We proceeded in that way for the first month, three times a week. Our familiarity grew; she shared her misgivings and began taking me into her confidence. She was engaging me in a romantic psychotherapeutic relationship, while I continued to focus on her physical improvement.

She was always obedient in following my directives. But the tightening of her neck muscles whenever she moved was an indication of the enormous effort she was putting into controlling her movement. Still, even in the stiffening neck, her determination to please me was the dominant force. We can observe an infant's reddening face as they make the effort to do something that is still hard for them. There is a pressure added to effort that we still often stubbornly associate with working hard; as infants we somehow came to believe this sensory pressure is how something happens. When you see the same pressure/effort combination with adults, it suggests the stubborn persistence of this sense of will, the other side of a lack of sensitivity to the actual process of the effort. In line with that physical tension was her delightful sense of humor with which she was engaging me in a seductive game.

She had grown up speaking Yiddish, just as I had. Her father's first name was Yankel, which is also my Yiddish name. She made a point of bringing her father-in-law's book of Yiddish poems that her husband had printed and published. Our connecting in these ways was helping enormously with her physical improvement. Her seduction was a way of bringing me into her reality and an affirmation of her independence.

Once I saw that she was able to follow directions along with her constant assessment of where I fit into her fantasy of me, I began with what follows.

An important part of my approach to building up her strength involved working with her on standing. While she was bending her torso forward, I would use an open palm on the back of her neck to counteract the common tendency to initiate standing by lifting the head first forcing her to press her feet to the floor. After slow and repeated efforts over a few months, this exercise loosened the habitual tension in her neck, opening the musculature to *increase blood flow to the brain*.

It all hinges on remembering that the ground is our true *support*, and that our *feet are our primary contact with that support*. This *reverses* the usual invisibility of the body: our taking the body for granted as what follows our intentions is a common illusion based on an early unconscious denial of what truly supports us. Most people stand up by lifting their head as if this pulls them upward, as if the body follows their intention through the eyes' reflexively; a will abstracted form the body like this is a form of magical thinking. Magical thinking originates in the child's discovery of the incredible power of thought.

As both a psychoanalyst and a creative movement teacher I was able to negotiate our work together. I made her work physically while she made me work psychologically. We were both winning on the score of who was in charge of the relationship. I was helping her to walk and she was indulging her fantasy, her self-image of being seductive and independent.

Within four or five months she was able to walk holding on to my fingertips with barely any loss of balance. Her habit of repeating herself vanished with some other symptoms of Alzheimer's, as she regained the moxie that had characterized her impressive lifetime of achievement. She had been the chair of a number of organizations, travelled the world, married and raised three children. She had been a woman capable of holding her own, seemingly without needing the approval of others.

After we began our work together, at a Sunday dinner with her husband, son, and daughter-in-law, she triumphantly told her husband, *"You have your affairs, now I have mine."*

The stroke told her, "You can't." Her fantasy announced at the dinner table said, "I can." Muscles that wouldn't, became muscles that could. Her repressed anger with her husband played a contributing part in her stroke, denying her passionate body; this was effectively *reversed* as she regained her connection of *mind and body – mind commanding body.*

We all forget the inner undivided, sensory kinesthetic experience of the muscles as we gain kinetic mastery over our physical and psychological relationships. Even though the muscles are like the breath in being fundamental to our physical being, they work so automatically to support our intentions that the sensation of their presence, though not totally repressed, is not consciously acknowledged. It is only when they don't work that the work our muscles have been doing all along becomes conscious; alarmed, we run to the doctor, swallow pills, undergo operations. But none of this puts us in touch with the actual process of *motion through muscles.*

We understandably try to get rid of pain to reinforce our sense of control, but treating only symptoms is a continuation of magical thinking, *reversing* the emotional terror that physical pain evokes; there ultimate fragility of life that infants experience with such urgency is contained in our relation to pain.

Megan moved across the studio space with a lightness that made the other women envious, with an envy that was often unconsciously *reversed* into admiration. No one else came close to the breeziness with which she moved. She didn't seem to bear the heaviness of life's complications in her body, a heaviness that the others could not escape while improvising. She was lighter than wind, more like light.

I was struck by the thinness of her movement, how it had no tactile texture, no bodily depth, as if there was no musculature to impede her spirit. I saw motion without feeling, a runaway soul without a physical body. Her dancing was an unconscious act of omnipotence that left her unbounded. This woman was a scholar. Her mind was full of references that earned her a Ph.D. Her character was defined by how determined she was to organize and to understand.

Her obvious enjoyment, combined with the group's admiration of her, presented an imposing force. I cautiously asked that she sense her feet on the floor as she moved. Her paying attention to sensing her feet on the ground made an immediate and palpable difference and was emotionally evocative for those of us watching her. Her aesthetically refined denial of the aggression of the body in motion came through. We witnessed her strength and determination. The runaway soul became a physical presence with power. Her soul found the instrument that makes music.

That last sentence is loaded. "Aesthetically refined denial of aggression" translates as: she unconsciously managed to make a charging five-six-foot tall body, running through space appear "lighter than the wind, more like light." She was not a heavy person. But an adult sixty-year old woman running through the space of the studio is an object that can knock you down, something that I think it's fair to call *aggression*. And yet, her body appeared "lighter than wind." Her aggression is unconsciously denied and reversed. This was not something she was doing on purpose; it was an unconscious transformation. A magical lie. And then, by only suggesting that she pay attention to her feet, the aggression, and the force of this woman became visible, palpably sensed by all who were watching her. This is the sort of fantastic and genuine transformation that can happen.

Another citing of Reversal

Megan, a dancer, like most dancers, or like most psycho-physically immersed people (like Bailah), *used* her body from a fantasy perspective. From Megan's unconscious perspective her body was an omnipotence, closer to the divine than the human.

These people keep *using* their body and movements until injury strikes, or their aptitude fails them. In Bailah's case, the emotional upheaval of her rage was associated with her seeming omnipotent sexual physicality shockingly vanishing. These medical and emotional upheavals are *the consequences* *of inattention to the **process*** through which their control and mastery blessed their lives with achievements and gratification.

Another long-time student, Edith, was lithe and floated through space like unfurling gossamer. She also unconsciously evoked jealousy and admiration. For her, dancing was a sort of airiness.

In my effort, years ago, to have adult students experience their bodies more physically, I asked them to *Sense the weight of their body, their physical mass, as they improvised*. Most of the class were able to work in ways that approached what I was calling on them to do. Edith dropped to the floor in an almost mocking gesture, shouting at me, "Why do you want us to die? It's the opposite of what dance is."

I was shocked by her reaction. No doubt the rest of the class was also affected. I can't recall anyone else ever reacting in this way in any of my classes. She had shouted in dismay. It was an upsetting moment. She had always been more demurring, held back. I would like to think that I was careful in conveying what I meant by sensing *weight*, that I differentiated this sensing from being heavy, or becoming dead weight.

After the class, I kept going over what had happened. I recalled that she had suffered the loss of a much-loved father at an impressionable age. And his illness meant that for a number of years he was lying in bed like dead weight. Her airiness was an aesthetic *reversal* of the heavy pain of death, of her loss. Her airiness was her physical reminder, a somaticized expression of her weightless love for her father.

Her unconscious *denial* of the heaviness of loss was *reversed* into her experienced body of airiness as a celebration in the spirit of her love. This psychologically transforming reversal process allowed her to unconsciously treat all artists as somehow magical, mysteriously shining light on darkness. For her art floated independently of whatever was troublesome about the artist, separating the product from the underlying feelings of the artist as a person. This makes sense in light of the *reversal of denial*. She instinctively understood how her determined airiness transformed her tragedy. Her psychological defense, the *reversal of denial*, was, ironically, rigid. She was intractable in her belief in *reversal* and never managed to become the artist she wanted to be; she had lost the gravitas of her genuine feelings to an attitudinal performance of feelings. It is sad when something so wished for is never resolved.

The *reversal of denial* works until it collapses on account of the inattention to the actuality of the musculature through which action *must* work.

What Gets Reversed

In the previous section, *Denial Reversed*, I spoke about Bailah and how she related to me as the fantasy person she needed me to be. Her fantasy supported her independence of spirit and helped her to heal. I spoke about Megan's lightness, like a shooting star crossing the earth for seeing eyes to gaze in wonder. It wasn't just speed, but a way to feel independent. I spoke about Edith who knelt at the temple of art, lifting her spirit out from the heaviness of her loss and despair.

Their chosen ways of being independent involved distancing themselves from what was a too frightening a sensory intimacy. Their chosen protective shields were how they were split off from a direct connection to feeling. They reversed what to them was too dangerous to experience directly.

Bailah 85, suffered a stroke, and was repeating herself as a shield against her rage. Megan, lacked firmness, not in her mind struggling with a doctorate, but in her body hiding toughness. Edith carried the unhealed scars of looking at the object of love with whom she felt bound going to a place she didn't know how to follow. Their pain, their fear was more than they could bear, more even than what they could acknowledge.

Each one found, or unwittingly developed, a way to avoid the depressive grief and paralysis of fear. The fear was *reversed by its opposite.* Bailah overcame the consuming rage by recovering her pride, sensing her legs climbing the steps to symphony hall. Tentative steps, unfaltering as our fingertips touched never losing her balance. Megan's feet contact with the floor reinstated unmistakably the power she exhibited by flight with the strength of touching the earth without shame. Edith sensing the weight of her body made her realize how she could balance the vanishing spirit of loss.

The terror of suffocation is *reversed* by a demand for air, a rhapsodic love of breezes through the trees; the enclosing darkness of night is *reversed* by an insistence on space and on light. The threatening confusion of impulsive explosive behavior is *reversed* by an almost compulsive commitment to order, form, and safety. The inhibiting paralysis of panic is *reversed* into an excitement about rhythms, quickness, and by letting go.

These are *reversals* of terror into their opposites. These *reversals* are often defended passionately – "*I need light in the room and space to move.*" Or, "*It's hard to focus on my body when you play music with words.*" Or, "*I vant to be left ahlone!*" *Greta Garbo insisted.* These are statements made in a tone that does not brook contradiction. There is always more to these insistences than what the person so adamantly or cheerfully throws out.

Reversal often drives artistry and theory. The underlying emotional conflict propels an attitude about motion in space that is choreographically unyielding. Could panic strangling her gut possibly have dictated Martha Graham's *contraction and release* theory about the theatricality of movement, or Marlon Brando's gut-driven, sudden impulsive acting? These emphatic demands led as they aged, to Graham's severe arthritis, covered by arm-length gloves and Brando's shockingly blowing up like a balloon.

Donna, a patient, described her mother's thin, flaccid and arthritic body. She described the slowness of her mother's steps, carefully putting one leg in front of the other so as not to fall on her way from the bedroom to the kitchen, and spouting her thoughts as if all were listening to her, rather than looking worriedly at her.

How could little Donna not have sensed the disparity between voice and movement? This disparity permeated her childhood. Her mother sounded like everyone else, only more so. But her mother's motion was different from everyone else's in the household.

When Donna grew up, she enjoyed skating and falling on the ice. She thought that falling meant that she was going beyond her comfort zone – a reversal of her fear. She shows compassion in her interactions, but has trouble verbalizing sensations. This affects her ability to change, as if the emotional patterns she has laid down cannot be recalibrated. Her fear was buried, out of sight, without even a whimper.

Most people simply insist on their preferences for the activities they have chosen and have come to see as terribly important to them. *"That's who I am"* is not an uncommon affirmation, whether expressed harshly or light-heartedly. It is not unusual for individuals to become angry when they are questioned about their assertions; they feel that they are being judged or misunderstood. These reactions indicate a nerve has been touched.

It's difficult to analyze these *reversals* because they are protective of profound destabilizing emotionally laden sensory fears that hark back to perhaps preverbal memory when the body trembled, to a time before heaven and earth were separated.

The *reversal* gives a sense of control, of being in charge, of what is right about their wish. *The sensation is reversed, but the fear from which it sprang remains,* fueling the insistence, the superstition.

Change requires patience with one's self, requires kindness towards another, and humility about control, to unravel the mystery of dogmatic attitudes.

Sometimes, a serendipitous event borders on the miraculous. An elderly couple suffering from terminal heart conditions were paradoxically *reversed*. They had met at their cardiologist's office and fell in love. Their heart conditions disappeared. When the doctor was asked how this happened, he replied with a smile, *"We cannot explain this turn around medically."*

This *turnaround* is what sensitivity to the sensory muscular process, *becoming alive in motion,* will in time bring about. It is hard to explain this apparent miracle. *Denied feelings are reversed by tactile sensation,* by inhabiting our physical awareness. Denial of feelings is the psyche's defense against becoming overwhelmed by fear. Fear tightens muscle endings around joints, pulling into the skeleton, into an emotional paralysis.

Becoming grounded reinforces the brain's sense of balance. Overwhelming fear pulls muscle tendons inward and upwards, to an earlier more primitive level of support, into rigidity.

As the grounded sensation rises through the body the tightened musculature loosens, returning one's sensations to the body from which they originated. It reawakens the original connection of sensation and feelings. *Sensory reversals* that led to fixated attitudes or aesthetically hardened opinions begin to dissolve old fears naturally. The body is released from its incarceration, and its imaginary sense of control.

This practical physical grounded process can be put into play *anywhere and anytime.*

How the Body Splits

One thing you can't hide – is when you're crippled inside.
~ John Lennon

I play a disc by an Israeli group that has put the opening lines of Genesis to music:

B'reisheet barah Elohim et ha'shomayim v'et ha'aretz.
In the beginning God created the heavens and the earth.

The sanctity that these words have held over time, was given a fitting lyrical and melodic expression, like a folktale passed on in song through the generations.

Chava, my newest student is improvising with the *motion through the muscles* directive, a difficult exercise for a beginner. It is made even more difficult by her tight lower back, lifted upper chest, and limited flexibility through her buttock muscles. These patterned misalignments affect the *tactile* continuity of motion. She makes every effort to follow the directive, but her lowered head gives me the impression of her observing the body as it moves below her assessing mind. She is still not quite sure she is actually sensing the *motion through the muscles,* or maybe she believes she is in fact following the directive.

It is not easy to adjust to sensing motion passing through the muscles, especially *tactile* motion.

She is a bright woman, and exceedingly sensitive to our relationship. An example of how powerfully attentive she is to our relationship is how habitually she abandons standing over the flat of the heels with which I start the exercises. She turns her whole body towards me the very second, I begin to explain some new facet of the exercise.

As I have already mentioned, the adjustments to stand *symmetrically over the flat of the heels* necessitate minor, incremental and unique adjustments, because our perceptual process of contact with the floor varies from person to person. We begin the exercise by making these fundamental adjustments that initiates the incremental *tactile* realigning of motion from the floor through the muscles of the feet, calves, thighs, and pelvis. The *tactile* realigning demands increasingly greater sensitivity to the flow of motion dictating small torques, flexing of the knees, etc. I had repeatedly pointed out that once she establishes the placement of the feet and legs, she should try not to leave her placement in order to listen. And yet, she, unwittingly turns her whole body towards me like iron filings to a magnet. It remarkable how, in the moment she is unable to remember the precaution that I've repeated so many times and that she has, in some sense, clearly understood. She is a professional woman in her late sixties, a seasoned occupational therapist, with years of personal therapy, with grown daughters and grandchildren. It is bewildering.

It is unavoidable to treat her listening and understanding as *split off* from remaining focused on her own physical positioning. Somehow, listening involves a whole other level of relationship, a change in spatial orientation, lest it appear that she *is not really paying attention to me!* Her rearrangement of feet and body was so automatic that regardless of how often I would address her doing it or talk about it in different ways to convince her that it isn't necessary, she still did it!

The sensitivity to her body was separate from hearing me. Her ears dictated her body. She had to leave a continuing sensitivity to her own physical sensing self, to attend to me. My authority as the teacher unconsciously demanded leaving herself. You don't have to be a psychological wiz to realize that her unconscious habit must have started much earlier in her life. It had very little to do with me. She had been conditioned. Chickens, I recall working in a commercial hen building, keep pecking at the same place where the dish of water was placed even after the dish is removed.

These are fixated habits, emotional patterns *split off* from what is actually being physically sensed. Another example of the *mind body split*.

The difficulty in her effort to follow the directive of *motion through the muscles* was understandable to me from a psychoanalytic perspective. She isn't listening to me, but to some authority figure in her life that she paid, or had to pay, very close attention to; in psychoanalysis this is known as *transference*[6]. What I am teaching, to reawaken the perception of the body from the sleep it has been put into, is different from the "normal" way most of us grow up to experience and *control* the body. The *splitting* varies from person to person, but it is our general condition.

As *B'reisheet barah Elohim et ha'shomayim v'et ha'aretz*[7] keeps playing, my eye notices Chava lose the physical focus on the *motion through her muscles*. Her legs become stationary, supporting the minimally expressive upper part of her body. She is sensing her insides, which, ironically, have less to do with the body and more to do with what is going on in her mind. She is doing internally what she does when she turns towards me to listen. She doesn't know she has lost the *physical* focus. She shifted unconsciously into a relationship mode. Her *fantasy relationship* and body are split from each other. Her body continues to sway *as if* she is following the directive, she is *believing* she is dancing.

I stop the music, something I frequently do to share my observations in order to reinforce what might help the reawakening process of awareness, of inner kinesthesia – *motion through the elastic muscle strands*. I ask Chava, somewhat cautiously, because she gets flustered when I single her out, "Do you have a sense of losing your focus on the motion through your muscles?"

The startled reaction in her eyes confirms my supposition of her growing up with a *Look-at-me-when-I-talk-to-you* parent. She responds by immediately agreeing. Given her transference

---

6   Transference, Sigmund Freud, *Studies in Hysteria*, 1905
7   Genesis., 1:2, Yiddish-Hebrew bible, Abraham Dov-Ber Dvorkin

relation to me, taking me as an infallible authority, how could I be wrong?

She listens to the music in the same way she turns her body towards me when I speak, meaning that she tends to forget her sensation to the motion through her muscles. She sways to the music and punctuates the first beat of the measure that she hears as a natural demand. She does all of this quite nicely. It has the look of falling into a hypnotic seduction. It is all very sweet, but without any specificity in the movement. I have come to characterize this way of moving as *split off* from the *tactile* sensation of *motion*. Paradoxically, the person actually believes that they are experiencing what I can see that they are not.

It is all in their head. The mind is treating the *memory of motion as if* it is the same as the actual *tactile experience*. The body language does not express what she seems so totally immersed in, what she believes she is feeling. Her feelings are swirling round in her head, while the musculature is increasingly subdued, in order not to disturb the inner life of belief, her aspiring conjuring mind.

Her eyes are wide open, cautioning me to be gentle. *"Are you aware that you lost the connection to the musculature?"* "What happened?" I ask. She responds with, *"I began to listen to the words."* Her answer is right on, as if she knows the drill of being questioned and how to respond. And yet, *if she knows, why didn't she change? Is it because she can't or doesn't want to do anything about the pleasure of living in her fantasy of feelings?* Something is obviously not coming together.

Her orthodox Jewish background makes understanding the words possible and meaningful. Knowing a little something of her family background, I ask her who taught her the words.

"*My father*," she says, her voice is soft, obviously touched by uttering, "*My father.*" Then I ask her if the memory of her father teaching her somehow distances her from the body through which she is now trying to express her feelings.

My point is obvious to her, since she's heard me bring up, over and over, the slippery slope of losing the physical focus.

I have often pointed out that *memories, associations, and impulses*, sensed as originating from the body, in contrast to intuitions that we definitely think of as coming from the mind, can just as easily take us away from the reality of our muscular *presence*. It is the lack of the *tactile* that makes for the disparity, making the movement abstract and typical rather than specific.

The mind has the capacity to *split*, separate the body from the ongoing feelings flowing through the musculature. We become *split* without knowing.

Chava sensed the words physically, but the split-second in which she connected the words unconsciously to her father, interrupted her focus on motion through the muscles. She left her body for the *memory of love*. My description may sound strange and dramatic. But the quickness of these mental shifts can be observed in the body in motion.

The *splitting defense* is a natural unconscious somatic defense that we simply do not register; we don't recognize it as an emotional cutting off. Our mind treats the value we give to the words as if they are still connected to our feelings. When words and feelings truly mesh, they are powerful; this is the power of poetry or the resonance of a well-constructed sentence. Uncannily, something in us can *sense* the distance between words and feelings, their togetherness or separateness. My years of work with movement, has shown me that we can also sense the distance between movement and feelings.

I have been confirming this for years after it first became clear to me, wanting to make sure that it wasn't just my projected wish, but something everyone else was also feeling, seeing, sensing as irrefutable. I looked into it over and over, for years aware of how students might tend to simply go along with me their teacher.

The words conjured the memory of her father, like a spirit hovering within her. My question, *"Who taught you those words?"* and her answer, *"My Father."* made conscious how her conjuring mind unconsciously cut her off from her physical, muscular feeling process, shortchanging the fullness of her feelings for her father.

We, all of us, often do not sense the distinction between thinking and feeling, between illusion and reality. But, as the song says, *"One thing you can't hide – is when you're crippled inside."*

I have to share some things about *Chava* to let you in on what I knew. She had a profound respect for her deceased orthodox and learned father. She reacted to the words in the song like an echo from heaven. Her deeper, more personal feelings of love for her father could not yet be integrated into her flow of feelings. The thought of him and her feelings for him still needed to be separated, and thereby controlled, which the *splitting (defense)* in the movement demonstrated.

I asked her to return to her improvisation. *She continued to improvise, to express through her movement her delicate feelings towards her father without disconnecting the association from her body. The improvisation that developed was clearly more organic, more interesting from a movement language perspective. She **owned** her feelings of love.* It was deeply touching to look at her dance of love for a father who shared with her when she was growing up the resonance of the first words of Genesis, as if God himself was talking to her.

If we stay connected to the *tactile motion, our thoughts and feelings, our memories and feelings, our impulses and feelings remain connected, becoming fully expressive*. Great acting, great dancing, great musical performance is transcendent because of that connection.

Another student, *Madeline*, is a wonderful mover, incredibly sensitive to sound, like a bat. She doesn't just move she vibrates with the music. She is dynamically engaging. She also begins in earnest to stay with the experience of flow from the flat of the heels through her body in a loop of motion passing through the musculature. Suddenly, her hands begin to twist around each other like two enraptured snakes. It looked impressive, but her neck stiffened, signaling a *split*. The motion of her hands twisting around each other, like snakes twirling around the symbolic staff of medicine, the *caduceus*,[8] which is an elaboration of the single snake on Mercury's[9] staff.

Quickness is what most of us associate with Mercury, a quality that is particularly valuable for people who depend on having fast, glib tongues. This was true of Madeline, who has a quick mind. The quickness of the motion of her hands made them appear as if they were *split off* from the rest of her erect body, suggested the turmoil of an inner conflict. But why were her hands isolated? What were they symbolic of? Why did the rest of her body movement become stilled by the hands? Her dance took on more "meaning" than feeling. I wasn't quite sure

---

[8] *Caduceus*, the staff of the Greek god, Asclepius associated with healing and medicine.

[9] *Mercury*, a Roman god. Guide to the underworld. Patron god of finance, protector of merchants, shepherds, gamblers, and liars. etc.

what it meant at the time and didn't want to pursue this. Work with a student is therapeutic, but it is not therapy. There is a different contract between student and teacher.

I did ask her to stop after watching her for several minutes and tried to get a better sense of my own about what was going on. I asked her if she noticed how she got immersed in her hands. She is feisty and shoots back with, *"I just wanted to burst out from the straitjacket of the Interplay!"* She not only rationalizes her denial, but also diminishes the value of my directive. She is telling me by her retort to relate to her symbolic gesture, not her body and her feelings. The sharp tone and rhythm of her response convey anger being contained magically by the twisting hands, not unlike a puppet show of two people fighting with each other. The puppet fight shows the struggle, but because they are puppets, we laugh in delight at the make-believe performance.

A number of years ago I would have been arrested by the strength of her feisty retort. I would have felt rejected by this woman whose body excited me. Fortunately, my long experience with this kind of work, combined with a self-analysis that allows me to sense the other person's fear without recoiling, allowed me to respond with, *"O.K.! Why only through your hands? Continue without losing the sense of your feet."* The feet ground us.

She resumed her improvisation with a keener sense of how the motion through her feet was affecting her whole body. She moved more subtly as her whole body unfurled, expressing the more subjective complexity of conflict and defense, but also a longing for freedom, for space, for air, and the sensuality of involvement. We all enjoyed watching, and we complimented her on this much more personal expression of her feelings.

Madeline mistakenly experiences the aesthetic continuity of rhythms, gestures, shapes, and dynamics *as if* it is the whole of her. Her mind latches on to the sensations that are a part of her feelings, (see section on what gets reversed) *splitting* them off for the control of memory, possessing them with a compulsive resolve as if it is *"the truth, the whole truth and nothing but the truth."* What gets cut-off unconsciously is the excitement, the desire that is a part of her anger. The complexity of this mixed bag of feelings would somehow rob her of authority, of control. The *tactile interplay of muscles* was emanating this powerful mix that she has to learn to keep alive.

In the past, I would have reacted to Madeline's as if I was melting into the warm waters of the Caribbean, with no sense of her psychosomatic defense. I would have been seduced by the rhythms of her fluidity.

I recently heard another story of *splitting*. The woman, who told me the story was driving behind a car that was moving much too slowly, as if the driver ahead of her wasn't sure where she was going.

"I was getting increasingly annoyed by how long it was going on. I saw her directional signal for a right turn. Yeah, finally. I prepared to go around to the left as she turned right. In a flash, she begins a U-turn and smashes into my car. We both, of course, stopped. I started describing my version of what happened, to which she reacts by accusing me of impatience. Fortunately, a policeman pulls up, since it's an area where people speed, checks out the situation and tells her that she was at fault. I felt vindicated."

In response to this story, I comment that the other woman was so totally in her head, with eyes that did not see, and ears that did ☺ is is why I call the body the first responder to what we don't want to recognize. *The body is a diverter of feelings unless we learn to stay alive to tactile motion.*

CHAPTER 4

AWAKENING FROM FEAR

The Fear of Intimacy

> *... in my hand that draws... I very quickly sense...*
> *if there is any discord between us: between my*
> *hand and the 'je ne sais quoi' in myself...*
> ~ Matisse

Years ago, while working with my students I tried desperately to understand how feelings separate from movement, how the two split up and break apart. Based on what my students were telling me, I saw that this break was the result of falling into 'rabbit holes' opened up by unconscious triggers; memories, familiar music, unconscious impulses, anything that allows us to automatically fall into habitual emotional patterns and their specific accompanying physical habits. It is as if we are designed to break with our undivided embodiment.

I eventually came to realize that blaming these patterns was also a way of dividing mind from body. My explanation was that when the mind becomes preoccupied (with memories, musical associations, sensed impulses, and so on) it *splits off* from the body. Though my reasoning might have been sound, like most blaming, it did not effectively help to connect mind and body. My thinking was still trapped in polarities (mind/body, right/wrong, positive/negative).

What had, at this point, not yet occurred to me was that a more primitive rupturing was at work here: the birth of divisions and oppositions through *Me/You* or *Inner/Outer*. This birth of awareness begins during the first months of life. This is the beginning of *splitting*.

When a baby is sensing a change in their mother, a sudden shift, this is a sensory experience – the smooth in/out rhythm of breathing may be disturbed. How these early interactions play out shapes our sense of trust and distrust. Attachment Theory speaks of secure and insecure attachment. I am calling this feelings-connected or feelings-divided. It brings to mind God's dividing heaven from earth in the creation story in Genesis. A few years ago, reading this story in Hebrew, I discovered that God *trembled* after he made this first separation. The Hebrew word is *merakhefet*. I didn't recognize the word, so I had to look it up. I find it easier to imagine the infant trembling during the first *splitting* of "I" from "Thou," *earth*-self from *heaven*-Thou, the original break from the maternal all. Trembling made more sense to me than the Greek translation of *looking out over the void*. Observing the void seems too distant and sophisticated.

My experience with movement work takes me in the direction of recognizing the significance of our early life experiences as bodily real – twitching muscles, breath spasms, shivering skin, the mouth quivering. We are born with, and from within, this bodily language. It is our inheritance. It is our nature speaking a language we need to acknowledge and integrate rather than *split off* from, deny, avoid, and medicate. *The living body is the language of fear and wonder.*

We have to be grateful for the seventh day, when God rested from the work of creation. All of us need a day of rest to reconnect. The separations we labor under as human are too much for us to bear. Our birth in these divisions of "I" from "Thou" and "Here" from "There" leaves us divided from our presence. This *divisioning*, to coin a term, is also a process of reconciling; nothing is easily managed here.

The wholeness we have left behind can be represented in time as an idealized past; on a spiritual level it can be a destiny; on an everyday level it can be an obsession that is either destructive or practical. Throughout human history, the ways we have tried to feel totally connected are numberless.

The seemingly natural divisions, the differentiations we live with, are a *separation process*. "Divide and conquer" is a political strategy. Separating to conquer is a way of *controlling to rule*. Separating sensory experience from feeling allows this to happen. On the psychological level, it is a way to *control* our feelings.

A part of us is sealed off. To be carefully stored, protected defended, forgotten or denied. Some people seal off their love in this way. The splitting of our sensory life from our feelings affects our connectedness, distancing us from our own and the other person's experience. We hear what they say, but don't feel what they are saying. We may be able to sympathize while never reaching the point of experiencing empathy.

Newborns are naturally present, fully there with a caring *Thou* in the surround of light and darkness. Our connectedness began in the womb, where it was close to total. It remains a God-given sensitivity, without the inhibitions of consciousness, we sense without question and adjust without reservation.

As separation begins, the mother feels its incremental movements. This process of separation brings her joy over the infant's emerging self with the sadness of the distancing. How the enjoyment and sadness is shown makes all the difference in how the splitting is integrated. This is where all of us come from. A process so natural it is unremembered. Rekindling intimacy requires consciousness. Separation is unavoidable. Being respectful by accepting boundaries and not demanding agreement is essential, and maybe always an incomplete achievement.

The problem is that feelings are undivided. Feelings are not part of the world of isolated things, they are **presence.**

In my life, when I grew up, I thought that identifying as an artist and feeling strongly about issues insured my connectedness. Choreographing to express my feelings showed how much I felt in mind and body. I believed that the responsiveness of the audience to my creations testified to the depth of my feeling. The validation of the audience was seismic. I eventually realized that my experience was based on a deluded belief.

It finally became a question for me: Am I feeling or trying to convince? I began to wonder whether I was more mind than heart. Before these questions broke in, only hope and purpose mattered. What finally became clear was that *Me as you,* or *You as Me* is still a polarity, the form of my divided self. This divisive split infected my understanding like a virus, separating an idealized wish for intimacy that was more in my head from the longing in my heart.

One of my analysts persistently pointed out how readily I intellectualized, how for me naming the feeling was a way of objectifying the feeling and myself. I was not exactly denying the feeling, I was "short-circuiting" the resonance of the feeling, not letting the feeling breathe in its own time. I was taking the knowing, the awareness of the feeling and giving it a name as if this was the feeling itself.

However, learning about my unconscious defense didn't make this form of *splitting* fall away. It did temper my righteousness, but my understanding of what was, in psychoanalytic parlance, an *isolation defense* didn't effectively alter my emotional tendency.

Feeling, it seemed, was too much for me to bear. Naming was an exigency. The situation was urgent. I had to do something with my feeling, immediately, otherwise it was unbearable.

This sense of urgency was modulated over the many years I worked as a creative movement teacher and a practicing psychoanalyst. Then it finally disappeared during a class I was teaching in the early 1990's one evening when I saw motion and feeling merge in a student's improvisation. There it was: an indivisible and whole body/mind experience. I vibrated inwardly. I felt well before understanding. I felt fear, loneliness, excitement. I wanted to rush over to her, embrace her. I wanted to hold the body of wholeness. My desire was like an infant's needing the warmth and the contact of his mother. Thank goodness that by then I was able to tolerate separateness; I was able to respect the difference between the student's expression of feelings and my own. **But at long last, I experienced an empathy, a togetherness that didn't require speech or action.**

I began to see improvisational freedom as insistent gestures, controlled in turn by release and containment. What I saw in movement paralleled the emotional splitting I came to recognize in myself. I could see these bright adult students avoiding their feelings while believing that their movements were expressing them. They could talk about what they felt dancing, but they were not present undividedly in their movement.

Associations, memories, and impulses are a part of our makeup. To try to not be alive to them as they come up is an exercise in futility. The effort to push aside what is so intrinsically a part of our being and of the way we develop can't work out well.

Betty expressed this problem often: "I feel a constant struggle between the Interplay of Muscles and pushing aside my immediate way of reacting, of joining the music, my wish to move faster, to follow my impulses."

My instructions aimed at helping her were, she felt, merely slowing her down. She couldn't reconcile sensing the musculature with her sense of freedom. Her tendency was to split off into whatever caught her up; her sense of choice and freedom was determined by patterns that unconsciously held sway. Again, going against habits we do not separate from our being is an especially difficult task. Her improvisations involved constantly twisting and turning into her midsection; the language of her movements was pregnant with an incredible force. Betty was quick, smart, and fun-loving, but physically unfocused. My effort to bring to her attention the force that drove her physically inward merely fed her analytic sensibilities. She found how I approached her and how I spoke engaging. But focusing on sensing the interplay of muscles was beyond her. This went on for years. She kept coming to class because it *was* healing her lower back problem, easing her habitual inner tension, with "bon mots" and laughter.

Then, all at once, she sensed the motion clearly through the middle of her pelvis and torso, experiencing a natural flow of movement through her neck and fingertips for a quieter and fuller emotional experience. "I managed to do what I wanted without losing the Interplay," she said, in surprise.

Ordinarily, Betty visualized my descriptions and demonstrations, superimposing her visualization on the body. She seemed to do this at the speed of light. She also had a literary tendency; she was able to interpret my instruction metaphorically. As an example, when I talk about the motion of movement happening tactilely through the musculature, it registered to her mind as fluidity. She was a reader. Words were important to her.

Sensing tactilely involved giving up what was for her a core defensive trait. Asking her to relate to the tactile muscular sensation meant that she would be separating from me and focusing on her own physical experience. Fluidity, on the other hand, for her meant maintaining a connection with me and to what she thought I meant by *tactile continuity*. For her, what was of primary importance was that we were of one mind, rather than being two separate psyches with distinct ways of experiencing.

How significant each person's unique approach is has become more and more clear to me over the course of almost sixty years of working on these issues. She needed me to engage her relationally, which I am by my own native sensibility and through my cultivated professional awareness able to do.

Betty's tendency to concentrate herself in her middle body with twisting repetitive movements was a visible somatization.

It was as if she was treating her feelings as digestible. By physically controlling feeling as if she was *ingesting*, she somehow believed that she was handling what she takes in from the outside. The language of her movement didn't express her feelings, it portrayed her defense from feelings. You could observe the upper part of her body moving on top of her legs as if they were supporting columns.

A psychosomatic reaction, in Betty's case, in her middle, signals an unconscious resistance to letting motion flow through. The neck and fingertips of professional dancers are where this sort of concentration is more commonly seen. *When the formal elements of dance – form, gesture, line, space, and time – overshadow the kinesthetic interplay, feelings are being held back.*

I have witnessed a similar visible disconnect at psychoanalytic conferences, when the voice of the speaker unexpectedly changes pitch; the speaker has, unconsciously, shifted emotional gears. This is a situation where speaker and audience tend to gloss over the break that has occurred by remaining focused on the content of what is being said. There is an inveterate tendency here to disregard and coverup. Something has clearly happened to the speaker, the change of pitch in their voice was palpable. Of course, we do not know what it meant for them. Maybe it was an unintentional cover-up of a fear, as if their diaphragm momentarily stopped working. Do we join in the speaker's cover-up because we also don't want to feel fear? Are we mirroring the emotional defense?

I believe that this is a common way to avoid imbalance and the sudden unexpected emergence of fear that goes with it. Avoidance and denial strike in the blink of an eye. Suddenness can alert us to the possibility of denial.

Suddenness is associated with and reawakens our most primitive reactions. In any sudden break in experience that we register, we sense the loss of our natural connection with life. There is a final cutting off: we're left alone.

This in-born, psychosomatic reaction is part of our existential system. It allows babies to learn everything so quickly in the first two years of life. The encompassing wholeness of those first years reemerges when we fall in love. The impulsive movement towards a passionate embrace or kiss is an expression of this in-born system of connection. It breaks through our rational consciousness, awakening the frightening cosmic time that has been eclipsed by our adult sensibilities. Perhaps it is always here awaiting the sensory reawakening that allows us to emerge out of our aloneness.

When this capacity to sense another with such intimacy gets integrated into our very being, it becomes empathy. Needless to say, the integration is always subjective and charged and it requires courage.

Let me try to describe the light of this flame in the work of movement. After someone in class does their individual improvisation, one of us sometimes speaks about the break they noticed in the unity of the *interplay of muscles*. It's fascinating to hear each person's unique way of being in how they express themselves, in their manner and choice of words. Someone will worry about hurting the other person, and they may feel they have to flatter or compliment them for their passion; another will matter-of-factly describe what they saw the other person doing, believing that accuracy in the details of their report is a mark or demonstration of their fairness; another will make an effort to talk about the reason for the break, supplying a rationale, as if they are giving a gift. I can't recall anyone ever saying, "I felt your fear when your neck stiffened." Or "What happened to you? It was like a foreign spirit escaped with your soul. I got scared." We cover up the sudden breakthrough of fear in reactions of reversal, anger, dismissal, or arrogance. It all happens so fast.

We are generally careful about our feelings, and rightly so. Our own experiences with not being heard or with being misinterpreted, have cautioned us. But we can become careful to the point of not registering what we feel. If we speak unabashedly about our feelings it is often too adamantly, perhaps as a consequence of our repressed anger. We treat reactions as if they are feelings. But reactions are the residue of disappointments, of unheard feelings, of not being recognized.

What I have discovered over the years with my adult students focusing on *the interplay of muscles* is the natural emergence of feelings emanating through movement. At first, it surprises them. They experience a difference, but don't quite know how to grasp or relate to it. But they sense an unmistakable difference from their usual way of experiencing movement and dance.

The strong sense of feeling elicited by the improviser suggested to me that the contact with the ground, *the Interplay of Muscles continuing up through the body*, is the *now* of the body. The *now* does not exist in the objective world, in the structured world of meanings. The expression *"being in the zone"* describes the *now* as what it is, a way of being rather than the *knowing* we are used to. The *Interplay* is along the same lines as what Freud referred to as the *body ego*, it is present below consciousness. The *Interplay* allows our soul to experience the feelings of our thoughts, associations, memories, and impulses outside the range of *knowing* and *control*. When feelings and memory become profoundly connected, they are *mutually inclusive*. Body and mind are not two. The feeling of separation dissolves.

The body is the psyche's first responder, a seismic monitor of our core connected self.

The perpetual looping flow of motion through the body is what offers hope because it is presence.

Alone, Control, Letting go

It began in the winter of 1955 while I was stationed in Korea. The potbelly stove shut-off, I listen to the mountain lion paws on the snowy bank just above the shuttered Quonset hut window. I am inside, lying zipped up to my nose in my sleeping bag, alone and frightened. *What if the lion...* And, *Should I...?* — ricocheting thoughts off the cavernous walls of the mind.

The Quonset was assigned to me to set up a library for the battalion. Our Company was on the DMZ. The library was in the front of the Quonset, the back was my sleeping area. I read fifty-two books in three months, sipping scotch supplied by a friendly master-sergeant. I wrote letters to friends back home, giving myself in words to the distance between where I had come from and where I was now. There were very few replies. It turned out I was truly alone. The turmoil I was in was new to me. It was shapeless. There was this shapeless struggling with how I had moved away so thoroughly from my familiar world and self, into a more private space with loose boundaries, on the edge of existence. I remember clearly the times I spent waiting anxiously for when the scotch would make my eyelids heavy, and I would fall off into sleep.

I was starkly alone. The gnawing sense of dislocation centered on my lungs, taking me back to a singular asthma attack I suffered when I was five, and a death fear never consciously registered, and that I have never since revisited. Voices in my mind kept repeating, like a Greek chorus, "What are you going to do when you're discharged? What are you going to do? What are you? What are you?" There was no way of going back to what I was, to what I had been. The emotional body that was my childhood self, my teenage self, the person I was in my family, this body was dropping away. I was shredding the garment that had protected me against the coldness of being outside and alone in life. It was an emotional garment that until then I didn't even know was there keeping me warm. I shouted inwardly, shaking the walls of myself, "I will express my feelings and ideals as an artist." The chorus asked, "Artist of what? Artist at what?" It was the muscles of my body that shouted back, "A choreographer." A declaration that felt like trumpets blaring – movement, a language without borders, without words, speaking directly to the heart. What everyone, everywhere can feel and connect with. The gnawing stopped. The voices retreated. I was free. Alone. Resolute. Certain.

Recapitulating those endless weeks in these few short paragraphs gives it all a melodramatic cast. In fact, the period did have an operatic quality. Those difficult days and nights, the crushing loneliness, the powerful fantasy of being an artist, creating out of my own inner spirit. I was desperate not to fall on my face. I had never taken a dance class. I knew nothing about dance as art, beyond being rhythmically intuitive and having been praised for my dancing aptitude by friends and acquaintances. How was I going to make good on my grandiose declaration? I was floating over the dark murky waters of anxiety. I have come to think of murky anxiety as the amorphous space before the universe came into being or the "void" before the creation of heaven and earth.

Is that how it usually happens? I don't know. One imagines a wished-for-self, sensing a strength that cannot be dislodged, a line of action to be taken towards a goal that shines in the distance but is also what gives reality to the present. In this dream there is what bolsters hope and allows us to deal with fear. Can we so easily make ourselves believe? Lie to ourselves? Are we huddling with all the parts of our self against the cold terror of the murky amorphous waters? We perform these acts of defiance martially with trumpets, drums, and waving flags. Banners of our nation proclaiming, We KNOW – DON'T DOUBT raised high, silencing the tremors of the heart, with the clarion calls of belief, BELIEVE, BELIEVE, BELIEVE.

Where does all this consuming resolve come from? What got called forth out of the depths with such assurance?

Transitions

After our discharge from the army in Seattle, to celebrate our independence we drank, smoked, ate, and engaged in sexual adventurism; for me, sex was a choreographic act of intimacy. The tightness of my mind began to let go during this time.

My first piece of choreography was *Evanescence*, which was performed at a college workshop. Through this creative work the trembling heart of my childhood was disappearing into an active and creative power of symbolizing.

I thought that since dance was a performing art, learning about theater would prepare me for life as a choreographer.

From actors improvising on the steps outside a church, to Commedia dell'arte, to mystery and morality plays, to Shakespearian drama, all the way up to Michael Chekhov's theatricality – I was fascinated by these historical transitions. I studied acting and directing and stage design, and learned how to build, paint and light sets. I was becoming equipped for a life in the theater, a serious business celebrating the art of make-believe

What *can* release us from aloneness? Can choices make us feel unconfined?

Along with the GI bill, I supported myself by teaching Yiddish, my first language, along with Spanish, and Hebrew. I was also teaching Jewish history in after-school programs. My sectarian past, overshadowed by my newly minted universality, was still coming in handy.

To celebrate an adventuring manhood, I choreographed *Afternoon of a Faun* to *Carmina Burana*, Carl Orff's only orchestral piece.

After two six-week summer programs at the American Dance Festival (1957- 58) in New London, Connecticut I was exposed to the luminaries of the avant-garde of Modern Dance: Jose Limon, Martha Graham, Alvin Nickolias, Murray Lewis, Merce Cunningham, Helen Tamaris, Doris Humphrey, and Louis Horst. This experience allowed me to hone my aesthetic sense. I entered the dance diploma program at Juilliard in 1958. At twenty-four, I was rather late to be doing this by most standards During this period my devotion to cultivating technical skill was overshadowing my aloneness.

The classes I took were consuming. Three hours a day of ballet, Limon's Modern technique, dance composition, dance notation, music and long rehearsals in a concert folk dance company – burning calories, dissipating my ill-defined anguish. In all this I was taken over and informed by the drive to control, as if realization was attainable only through perfect control of the body. This seemed the one path to becoming the artist I imagined I had to be. The total immersion felt definitive, removing the underlying doubts that frightened me into my decision in the first place. Doubts pushed aside, to be answered much, much later.

One of my first jobs in New York was teaching Modern Dance to children at a parent-teachers co-op in Kew Gardens, Queens on Saturday mornings There was a little seven-year old girl with a healed broken hip who was scared to let go of her crutches. I helped her to run freely along with the other children over the course of a few months. After my class, her parents were overjoyed to have their little girl back, no longer terrified.

I am praised for my teaching talent at the end of the program's celebratory luncheon. Asked about my approach, I describe what I had done with the students and how with this little girl I, little by little, lowered her feet onto the ground for her to learn again to experience trust. There was no pedagogic design beyond my wanting the children to have fun. I felt ashamed of my lack of serious pedagogic thinking. My natural sensibilities seemed inadequate to me. I was shifting, without really knowing I was, from being an artist/choreographer to becoming a dancer and teacher.

Certainty

By the end of the year at Juilliard, I concluded that the difference between just dancing and professional dancing is *having an internally imaged sense of whole-body form.* Form was, in my mind, the *sine qua non,* of every dance technique. The dancers praised in classes all had this sense of form. Their body and movements always had this special unified look, with their gestures coming alive. The living connection of their performance was breathtaking.

My guiding idea of achieving control in order to *let go* was becoming cemented. Many years passed before I was to discover my soul didn't quite accept the equation of control as the way of deliverance from the internally huddled tightness of being alone.

My guiding idea of achieving control in order to *let go* was becoming cemented. Many years passed before I was to discover my soul didn't quite accept the equation of control as the way of deliverance from the internally huddled tightness of being alone.

While still in the grips of my attachment to form, I stumbled on a problem-solving framework that combines control and 'letting go' in a creative way. In one of my classes, seven-year old, Jeffrey Kern danced *clay.* I had asked the class the previous Saturday to think of something heavy and to show how it moves in their improvisation. Most of the improvisations were short-lived and uninteresting. Jeffrey's clay improvisation was stunning. I was stunned by his performance. Every gesture he made and every shape he formed himself into, and there were many, was held together by the feel of the specific heaviness of clay. He never, for even a second, stopped moving like clay or looking like clay. It was astonishing both to me and the accompanist who was a piano major at Juilliard. We just looked at each other in wonder.

My analysis of why this performance by this student was so much more effective than all the other improvisations eventuated ten years later in the book *CREATIVE MOVEMENT FOR CHILDREN: A Dance Program for the Classroom* (1969, Van-Nostrand-Reinhold, co-authored and exquisitely designed by John Lidstone, the director of the Kew Gardens program). John's uniquely convincing photographic exposition of my creative movement discoveries was so impressive that as the six thousand initial printing circulated abroad, it brought people from around the world for teacher training summer workshops to The School for Creative Movement. I founded the School in 1962, which grew, with the public relations talent of my ex-wife, Hattie, from 38 six and seven-year old to 210 children, 3-15 year old, plus 150 adults by 1972 and a staff of ten teachers. The staff grew, when we combined art and dance classes, correlating the creative art explorations with the successfully working dance curriculum, all arranged by age group. The art program worked under the guidance of Mary Newhouse, a wonderful, talented, generous, artist with marvelous, inventive skills.

In taped interview that John, my co-author, had made with seven-year old Jeffrey, John asks, "What do you think is the greatest thing that dance has taught you? What is the real secret – that it has given you?" Jeff doesn't hesitate for a second, "Feeling – the whole secret is feeling."

My eyes welled-up with tears when I listened, when I heard these words, "Feeling, the whole secret is feeling." How did this seven-year old arrive at his insight into movement and feeling? I wasn't working on feelings. I certainly couldn't own that I was. I was doggedly focused on teaching form, which I had so proudly concluded was the ultimate goal of teaching dance. I never forgot Jeffrey's saying straight out: *Feelings – the whole secret is feeling.*

My analysis of the impressive clay improvisation solved the riddle of *control to express, while letting go.* I developed age-appropriate improvisational foci for children over the course of fifteen years, into curriculums for each age group three to fifteen.

I maintained my authority as guide, and visionary, able to evaluate conformity or resistance, pleasure or confusion, commitment or indifference. Six-year-old Alan Gilbert, to become the celebrated conductor of the New York Philharmonic, grasped the essence of the images combining form and quality like the instrumental coloration in a musical score, with remarkable clarity. Little Eddie Shellman, a few years earlier, who became the principal dancer of The Dance Theater of Harlem and an international ballet star, made the improvisational study of *rubber band* look easy. *Rubber band* was the image I used to explore the quality of lightness that the elasticity of a rubber band elicits. Years later, backstage after seeing him in the leading role in *Scheherazade,* he tells me that he used the *rubber band* image as the core movement quality for his character in the ballet.

Children identify and totally believe what they are trying to be. Identification is central to their sense of play, to learning, to discovering what engages them.

Adults were a problem. They have experienced too many ups and downs, too many doubts, disappointments and failures. Their longing to *let go* led from the traditional following of steps and movement phrases, common in professional dance classes, to creative explorations with *letting go*. I began by trying to affect *breathing,* noting their physical tension just listening to me in anticipation for doing what was expected. I asked them to run around the studio adjusting their breathing till they sensed that it was in sync with the music. The musical selections varied from Vivaldi, to Jane Olivor, to Olatunji's Nigerian drums. The willingness to consciously allow their breathing to alter liberated them from habituated unconscious emotional patterns. Breathing constantly changes in response to whatever we are doing and feeling. Since breathing is handled mostly by our autonomic nervous system, we don't have to think about it; the awareness of what they were doing to sync breathing, running, and sound, made them realize how much habituated breathing patterns are an unconscious form of *control*. This is why attention to breathing is so fundamental in meditation practices, as a beginning process for awareness. The improved looseness in their bodies and the smiles on their faces showed me that they *were* letting go. It turned out to be an easy explorative teaching technique, and fun.

The freedom of running reinforced the essence of movement. Running, and then improvising to varying pieces of music, the essence of creative movement, was dance, without following steps. However, their gestures and shapes remained too general, lacking specificity. To enhance a more specific internal physical experience I followed the breathing explorations by the sensing of motion. Exploring motion not as moving through space, but as the sensation of motion through the body. To elicit this inner sense, I asked them to run counterclockwise in a circle with the left arm outstretched, body slanted, and eyes focused towards the center of the circle. Doing this for a several minutes becomes somewhat hypnotic, as the sensation of motion is internally evoked. I then asked them to sense the sensation passing through every part of their body. Some found this difficult; it was as if the external and internal must remain separate. Something has to be walled off. Something must not be penetrated.

It was confounding to realize that some people make no acknowledgement of *motion* as an internal physical sensation They proceed as rational, with their focus on the speed of their intent through space, on their assertive moving self. This exploration went on for numerous weeks with varying pieces of music. The repetition with different music was to prove to them that it is their *awareness of motion* passing through their body, rather than pushing through space, that elicits their feeling of dance, their connection with the music. The technique will be addressed in a later piece.

Continuing to stress how much of their awareness of *sensation* is essential to their experience of dance, reinforced their physical options. I began to recognize that the *physical awareness of sensation* serves adults in the same way that *identification* serves children. It elicits the same psychological freedom as imagination does for two and three-year-old.

I continued with what I had come to believe as the next base element of dance, *beat*. I approached it by stepping on each *beat*, once again with varying music. This eventually led to standing in place keeping the *beat* with the feet, then shifting to only knees, then only hips, continually isolating the beat in body parts, then only the thumbs, and finally, to standing totally still while the *beat* continued to pulsate in the head. It becomes obvious that beat is memory, and memory is time, yesterday, today, tomorrow.

On a more personal level, I understood that Memory is my father's hope. Memory is control of imagination.

Beat makes the band step in unison. Beat brings the tribe together, eighty-year-old dancing in a circle with three-year-old. These explorations affected their sense of time, allowing them to see how time is malleable and how fixated emotions are habituated time.

How we experience our physical selves can alter our inner lives. I was connecting *sensation and memory* to make them experience *the dancers they wished to feel like*, not as a wish, but as an *awareness of sensation* inherent in moving.

Improvising with the sensory experience of *breathing, motion,* and *beat* brought descriptions of movement in space and time into a more conscious personal sensory experience, facilitating the letting go of habituated patterns of dance.

Freedom is at the heart of all movement. Exploring spatial possibilities is what Modern Dance was about, in contrast to the verticality of ballet. Modern Dance eventually influenced ballet choreography, in the same way that impressionism, cubism, influenced all subsequent art.

Because improvisational dance has no right or wrong movement, gesture, or shape, individuality is implicitly more pronounced.

One particular class became a seventeen-year movement therapy group in which I shared my thinking about the nature of these explorations. The group eventually developed into focusing on movement interactions with each other, followed by verbal exchanges about their physical experiences, evoking a 'group therapy' sense of intimacy. Movement is such an early part of our human development that sharing it with others in combination with talking evoked a strong sense of intimacy.

Something is Wrong?

Inventing explorations for *letting go*, helping individuals overcome resistances, was fraying my *controlled aloneness*. The disparity between my own integration of movement elements and my personal psychological development wasn't necessarily doing the same thing for the students. In addition, by 1980, other personal issues moved me to enter into psychoanalytic training to learn about why it is so difficult to *let go*, when it is so powerfully wished for.

I was treating *letting go* and *control* by focusing on the awareness of breath, motion, and beat with beginners; shape, gesture, *impulses within gestures*, to experiencing weight, to enhance the physicality of the body with intermediate level students; then exploring *time* and *space* through *four distinctive centers* and *seven different breathing placements* with advanced level students. All the techniques for exploring these movement elements were my own creative pedagogic inventions.

All of these sensory experiences affect fear. The inhibiting, paralyzing experience between body and mind was becoming clear to the students. However, awareness of sensations is therapeutic, but it is not awareness of feelings. Sensations accompany feelings, but they are not feelings. I could see and join in the delight that they felt, but their movement language remained rather limited. The explorations were liberating the mental inhibitions but not eliciting the complexity of feelings, a freer more complex, more subjective movement language.

Something was missing in my thinking about creative movement. I was undergoing a transition from thinking that the essence of dance is *form,* to realizing that feelings are the core of what I was trying to evoke for dance be truly alive.

In the former, I was treating *letting go* of the body as an object, an imaged, controlled object that we need to *let be.* I was contrasting *control and letting go,* a way of thinking, rather than getting them to experience what is actually working, the **muscles.** I was treating *sensation* as thought rather than an experience that is going on to which we put a word. I was using the *memory of* bodily experiences to release feelings. I was dealing with *what had happened,* and not with *what is happening.*

I felt like Galileo realizing that the earth turns around the sun, not the sun around the earth.

A Turning Point

In keeping with my unconsciously determined *aloneness,* I was now reclaiming a more related sensibility, acknowledging what actually is working when we move our **muscles.** The more attention I paid to individuals and their *muscular alignment* problems, the clearer it became that **the tactile motion through muscles** is what needs to be awakened for a more specific and subjective movement language to come through in improvisations. It was this understanding that led to the fundamentals: 1) contact with the ground, 2) the 4th toe line placement, 3) narrowing the stance, 4) shortening the stride, 5) to the interplay of muscles; and eventually to the significance of 6) the flat of the heels, and 7) the loop of motion through the interplay of muscles.

Muscular alignment must be *nurtured,* rather than, as commonly demanded in traditional dance techniques, *positioned.* There is nothing wrong with ideal postures, or concepts about optimum flexibility or strength. However, dance must be *nurtured through alignment,* and *alignment through an awareness of and sensitivity to* **tactile sensation**. When it is not, injuries ensue; and postures may appear impressive, admirable, and even suggestive, but they are unfeeling.

This changed my approach to stretching and strengthening exercises and to the creative improvisational part of the class.

What makes teaching realignment difficult is that *control* and *habituated muscular patterns* are not only physical, they are also psychologically protective of our personal *fears and terrors.* Consider a baby's body cringing in the face of a jarring stimulus, whether from outside or inside. Our vestibular system (inner ear) is constantly monitoring instability, telling *muscles* what to do. Nature has constructed us to survive the *imbalance* of *fear.* The quality of experience has to be sought through awareness of specificity, whatever the discipline.

As this understanding became clearer to me, psychoanalysis and creative movement began to dovetail. Internal and external fears are painful and they shock us. We learn how to handle fear, but we can't get rid of it, nor should we. It alerts us to the danger of crossing the street as cars whiz by. *Control* is inevitable. And although some people don't want to remember, *memory* stores experiences, giving us a control that allows us to process fear, and to create.

When control gets divorced and isolated from the fear it is managing, there is a problem. We lose a connection to our feelings, the source of our humanity, our moral compass. The sensate, receiving body adapting, not only to survive, but to love, begins to harden into memories of wished for dreams. We then look for ways of letting go. We end up living in a controlled, distrusting, divided self. We hope that our desires or ambitions will help us to let go. The split from our feelings is so common, so normal that it permeates our thinking, our theories, our lifestyles, our language, and our relationships.

In a recent class, Megan speaks a wish, "I would like to work on wanting and desire." It was a big order, to which I responded, "OK, I'm going to do this through beat, and rhythms." Electra jumps in, "This is going to be a hard class. You know how I feel about rhythms." Assuring her, I say, "I promise you an end to your struggle with rhythms." I was assuring them with unabashed confidence. The many years of teaching, discovering and understanding were expressed in my saying, "I'm going to do this through beat and rhythms."

I play music with a definite beat, repeating an exploration we have done many times over the years. I step, speaking out loud, *"One, one, one, one,"* as they follow. I stop to observe while they continue. I notice Electra getting mixed up. It looks like she suddenly reverted to her mental conviction, *"I can't keep the beat."* I stop the music to tell her, "Whatever thought comes to your mind, please do not lose sensing your feet." My instruction registers, she continues without a mishap. The thought took her away from her body as though thought and body can't be going on simultaneously. She totally got it. She understood how her holding on to the past creates the problem.

Megan has no issues with the beat but orchestrates it choreographically. I ask them to drop their *weight* into the beat, and demonstrate how this can be done. Electra has no problem with this. Not only is she sustaining the beat through her musculature, she is equally entering into the spirit of the beat. She has made a soulful connection with the music. Megan is having a hard time. She still needs to *control* the natural absorbing body.

"Stay with the interplay, make sure that it continually loops through the neck and back."

Megan's skilled, wonderful sense of motion now has a focus. Her control is organized *by the musculature*, rather *than the memory* of the beat, she tries to make *beat* interesting by choreographing. By following my suggestion, her movement language becomes more organic and evocative. She also recognizes how her mind creates the problem.

To accentuate how split-off thought divides us from feelings, I go over to Electra to move with her. Her eyes open wide wondering what I am up to. "Don't lose the continuity of the interplay, as we move together," I tell her. Our dance flowers as we improvise. Megan, looking on, comments, "That was a beautiful duet."

Fear, desire and awareness came together spontaneously. Maintaining the *interplay of muscles* allowed the erotic thoughts and feelings that came into play when I approached Electra to become a dance, rather than a sexual compulsion, or a defensive jerking away, or a repressed frozen body of paranoia.

Both Electra and Megan understood how sustaining a sensitive awareness *of the loop of motion that grows out of the interplay of muscles* is the energy of living.

In all fairness to the reader, I should add that both of these women had been students for many years. "Don't lose the interplay," had become an instruction they could put into play.

The letting go and control that rationalized my aloneness finally dissipated through my attention to the specifics of motion through the alignment of muscles emanating feelings. I could finally own seven-year-old Jeffrey's answer to John, "The whole secret is feeling."

Our Way of Life

Splitting, breaking feelings up into fragments until they obscure the felt experience, reversal and denial are unconscious psychological defensive operations. Our unconscious has this capacity for dealing with what we don't deal with, what we cannot accept emotionally, because it is too threatening – what is terrorizing and puts our survival into jeopardy.[10] It may appear to us as if denial, reversal, or splitting are consciously purposeful, but they are always based on fear. One of the telling signs of the underlying fear is how adamantly our defenses are expressed, verbally and physically; challenging these tricky defenses is emotionally trying, and can be experienced as disloyal. We start to teach our babies how to perform and see through these feeling cover-ups quite early.

One of the first games we play with infants is peek-a-boo. We are unconsciously teaching babies that shut eyes do not make what is in front of them disappear. Our baby's face expresses fear and then joy, as our face returns from behind our

---

10 *The Denial of Death,* 1973. Ernest Becker, Pulitzer prize in 1974. Becker builds on the works of Norman O. Brown, Otto Rank, Sigmund Freud, and Soren Kierkegaard.

hands. A traditional, inter-generational folk wisdom passed on so innocently. We all play this game with smiles and delight.

Although we ask for evidence in court and in science, there is a part of us that believes or doesn't. We sense more than what we are able to see, hear, smell, taste or touch. We have to be touched emotionally, touched not by a sensation but by a current that runs through our whole body. It is that current of motion that I call *The Loop of the Interplay of Muscles*. Outside and inside mesh on a personal level that runs through us like a river. Describing it can never reach the personal experience.

Soldiers who develop post-traumatic disorders obviously are having a horrific time processing their experience, the shock of what they have undergone and witnessed. There is something about these horrors that threatens their sense of emotional wholeness, their sense of sanity. It's hard enough for young adult soldiers, let alone young children. The mind finds it hard to process "un-wholeness." The mind works on keeping things together, that is what feeds our survival and eventually our pride. The experience of chaos leads to a sense of madness. It is unsettling for the mind and unbalancing for the body.

This is why wishes and beliefs are so strong, even in the face of contradictory evidence. Let me share with you a sweet example of covering up what is being expressed.

I recall overhearing a father in the dressing room after a dance class talking to his dawdling three-year-old who was not getting dressed, "You're making me climb the wall," to which she responded, "Oh, Daddy," with a chuckle. She simply couldn't register his anger, although he said it with a humorous flippancy. The "Oh, Daddy," conveys her being in love with daddy, her needing him to be grounded and be a source of safety. She was not prepared to interpret his "climbing the walls," as an expression of his feeling that he was losing his sense of being grounded. Acknowledging his anger would be too emotionally traumatic for her. Children, especially toddlers, do this all the time. Mother yells about something. The toddler gets scared, as if looking into eyes of Medusa, and cannot believe that the woman who two minutes ago embraced and kissed the top of their head and cheeks is yelling, so they make up a wicked witch. They *split* their mother in two and have no doubt there are two separate people. It is so natural and common an event that we as adults are charmed by it. We celebrate it in fairy tales, and multi-million-dollar, blockbuster movies.

Dorothy (Judy Garland) in the *Wizard of Oz* sings after her aunt Emma tells her to "find a place where she won't get into trouble." "A place,' Dorothy repeats again and again in a sort of hypnotic rhythm, *'you can't get to by boat or train."* It was a lead in to singing, "Somewhere over the rainbow/ Way up High/ There is a land that I've heard of /Once in a lullaby." Written in 1939 by two Jewish guys, Harold Arlen (Hyman Arluck) and Yip Harburg (Isidore Hochberg) from orthodox or left leaning immigrant parents from the Lower East Side of New York, raised understanding the wish for hope of Jewish immigrants happy to get out of miserable, threatened lives in Poland and Russia, and the overcrowded Lower East Side. Dorothy spins away through a stormy chaotic whirlwind to the Land of Oz and finds her way home by clicking her heels – wake-up clicks, shifting her awareness from imaginative wishes to contact with reality, her feet on the ground.

Children do this in a slightly different way. I recall standing on Broadway and ninety-second street waiting for a bus to go uptown, seeing a seven or eight-year-old behind me pick up a small torn piece of white paper, lift it onto a slanted architectural ledge that ran along the bottom of the wall, vocalizing a car motor rumble while moving the scrap of paper along the ledge. He was a poor boy, it seemed to me, but how wonderfully imaginative, I thought, thinking back to my own childhood in old Havana with no toys.

We not only transform pieces of paper, *split* what we like from what scares us into two different objects, but equally *reverse* the loss of rotting flowers into the aesthetics of impermanence, which the Japanese call, Wabi-Sabi,[11] a quite beautiful aesthetic.

Freud introduced *reversal* in his dream interpretation, as in the fear of climbing stairs to who knows where, *reversed* as descending the stairs into the bosom of love; or, going into the murky water *reversed* as coming out of the water, rebirth, or a baptism.

Reversal serves as a solution to frightening feelings.

To show how common this mental process is Freud cites single words that have opposite meanings. Every language uses words and expressions in exactly this sort of way. Consider how love/hate and sadism/masochism are two sides of the same coin. My French wife uses the expression, "The chocolate cake is to die for." There are many examples, but these will suffice.

Edith was a perfect example of this reversal. In her mind her father's death was a dead weight; she reversed this into its opposite, lightness. Ted reversed the debilitating slowness of his medical impairment into his quickness of spirit and humor.

---

11 The Japanese aesthetic of Buddhist teaching, nothing lasts, nothing is finished, nothing is perfect, that is its beauty.

Bailah, like a consummate actress, shifted her traumatized and unresponsive eighty-five-year-old body into the fantasy of having an affair

It seems intuitively obvious how these *reversals* can transform our impotence, turning situations we cannot deal with into something else. We have all *done* this unconsciously. I can imagine the three people I cited scoffing at my assertion of their unconscious *reversals*. I would be accused of psychobabble or mumbo jumbo and arrogance regarding a way of life they have found invaluable.

We can do the same with our kinetic skills, *reversing* the kinesthetic body rattled by fear, love, or loss, into physical ambitions – maybe jumping higher than anyone else, lifting off from our earthbound life like a bird, or escaping from the terrible maze, like Icarus[12] before his fall.

We participate in cultural *reversals* of fear, pain, anxiety watching or playing sports. Cirque du Soleil provides us with countless aerialists defying gravity. We can identify with them without giving this unconscious process a second thought.

Splitting and *Reversal* are essential to our self-protective fabrications from the beginning. Against our terror and vulnerability and impotence as infants or adults, intolerable fear is stood on its head by becoming the thing feared.

Reversal is expressed in our personal family theater with our parents. We blame them for our frailties, and just as easily become them. Our disowned natural sensitivity becomes a psychological tennis match with people we love and hate.

---

[12] *Icarus,* son of Daedalus the inventor of the Labyrinth imprisoned by King Minos of Crete, created wings of feathers and wax for himself and his son to escape from the tower. Icarus flew to close to the sun melting the wax and fell to his death.

Airiness, lightness, quickness, dullness, slowness, heaviness, hardness, are woven into our physical carriage and aesthetic values. Professional dancers often mistake defined control of intention for feelings. Analysis, like direction in space, is orienting, but analysis is not the inner motion, the vibrating experience, or the more encompassing silence of feelings. Critics interpret the *reversals* of our creations for the public as best they can.

Henri Matisse in book *Jazz* (color paper cutouts with handwritten text) wrote eloquently about the awareness of what can and does happen: *"If I have confidence in my hand that draws, it is because when I was training it to serve me I resolved never to let it overshadow my feelings. When my hand is paraphrasing my feelings, I am very aware if there is any disagreement between the two of us: between my hand and that indefinable part of me that seems subjugated to it."*

Matisse's words are exactly what I am talking about; our movement must never disagree with that *"indefinable part of"* us that is our feelings. We **can** learn to sense *"any disagreement between the two of us: between my movement and that indefinable part of me..."*

CHAPTER 5

PRACTICALITY IS HOPE

The Odyssey to Muscles Discoveries and Insights

Overview

What I have discovered and am sharing with you are exercises that can be carried out by anyone. They are incredibly practical. The accounts I offer are meant to serve as landscapes for you to enter. The examples are to help you apply specific suggestions. The accounts and stories are also meant to allow a space for reflection on habit and give you feel for, and sense of, why our habits are so hard to change.

On a personal level it has been my journey over these many years to find an ongoing sensed-feeling-awareness through the body to my father's muscles as he played out the rhythms of a train, tapping his feet while slapping his chest, making the Choo-Choo sounds of a train. My father instilled in me the joy of rhythms, their sounds, the pleasures of a body that could play.

My professional discoveries led to the *Loop* of the *Interplay of Muscles,* a chrysalis in which physical motion emerges as timeless feelings. Most of my teaching foci appeared or developed logically, some totally unforeseen became undeniable.

In the Beginning

I began my professional journey with the same assumptions most people make about the body and movement – flexibility, strength, and control – the practical triad underlying imagination, creativity, intentionality. This was the soil tilled for physical skills, choreographic inspiration, theatrical directorial ventures, and for a life of teaching and founding The School for Creative Movement. This trinity of *flexibility, strength,* and *control* pretty much dictated my personal training in a variety of modern dance techniques, from ballet to jazz and Afro-Cuban.

About Children and Adults

Young children, as well as untrained adults, have a generalized sense of the body. It's simply there. But it's so close to them mostly as an imagined body: *what is transparently available to them, what they act and are expressed through.* The natural course of growing up facilitates separating parts of the body: neck, fingers, arms, upper torso, pelvis, and legs. Consequently, beginning exercises are generally dictated by warming up these gross body parts, by activities that stretch the muscles to enhance the freedom of flexibility. Usually the head and torso are stretched as one, and pelvis and legs are stretched together. Usually, strength activities, like sit-ups, focus on abdominal muscles, or the holding power of muscle endings that connect to joints. As children age, exercises become increasingly more specific; with adults, also, exercises are separated by how the parts of the body connect. The flexibility of the spine, torso, and legs depends on how far out into space any part is able to reach. Strength is tested by how long in time any part is able to be held. This generally also is the standard approach for most dance techniques.

Commentary

This standard development and professional dance technique approach reinforces a skeletal imaging of the body: a visualization of the body, seen from a ghostly *outside*. An example of this view from the outside is focusing on how far away from the body into space we can stretch. Since the muscles connecting to the joints are the tightest, the effort is to open the joints for maximum flexibility. The irony is that the more the joints are opened by stretching muscle endings, the greater, eventually, will the person sense the need for muscular strength to hold that part of the body up. In time, the connection of muscle tendons to bones is weakened. Added to this weakening of the body is a pulling at the ligaments, the wire system between bones. Psychologically, since muscles suspend bones, overstretching them is unconsciously a negation of the body's inherent unifying structure. Overstretching some muscles more than others unwittingly fragments the connective interplay between muscles. A mental consequence of this unconscious fragmentation results in imaging how it all fits together, how it did, or should fit together. The idea of *Form* replaces our natural inner kinesthetic experience of unity. Control of *Form* becomes central in the way we think about our experience and judgment of movement.

People simply do not realize that their musculature may not be by nature able to withstand this sort of treatment. This sort of repeated overstretching leads to joint replacements for so many dancers, athletes, and anyone who taxes their body to conform to the 'ideals" they have in mind. Individuals not naturally endowed for the strains of these demands overwork the skeletal musculature, weakening the connection to the bones, and suffer injures or, hopefully, self-protectively drop out.

I continued in this general approach to exercises, focusing on flexibility, strength, and control, into the middle 1980s, whatever inventive ways or various techniques I tried. But then, individual considerations began to loom larger than my idealized instructional aims.

The second part of most dance classes involves a combination of steps in ballet or choreographed movement phrases chosen from the choreographers' repertoire. These combinations of steps, body shapes, directions and timing are practiced repeatedly increasing in difficulty from beginners to advanced levels. Talent is measured by how well the individual melds these combinations to convey their emotional sense.

I can still remember Jose Limon, who had a rather large upper chest, demanding that I extend my chest out, making me pull my shoulders upward, and the contrast of his approach with my ballet teacher's, Antony Tudor, telling me to drop my shoulders. These back-and-forth directives went on for the year at Juilliard. No one ever spoke about the musculature. The muscles were expected to conform to the demands of these postural directives, as if the image of structure dictates the *how*, of function. This is a classic aesthetic argument in architecture; and in the Arts, the isolation of *technique* and *expression* has been the rule. Implicit in this understanding of *technique* and *expression* is a reinforcement of the skeletal/conceptual model of the body, because *expression* without the unity that structure organizes for motion looks sloppy. Form, the sharpness of joints, strikes us, visually, as a unity or togetherness. Children's stick figures symbolizing mommy and daddy are almost always drawn with big eyes and the ends of the lines representing legs and arms are connected to the torso as joints: this shows our primitive image of the self as externally connected. The oversized eyes are a symbol of awareness, if being seen and connected with – being loved or controlled – through seeing and being seen. Most of us tend to develop the skeletal model because it's easier for the mind to remember the moving connections as joints rather than the *tactile muscular continuity of motion*, which has to be sensed from within.

I discovered that children begin to consciously sense the elasticity of muscles by age eight. Earlier they are aware of muscles as tight and strong. The continuity of tactile motion through the muscles falls under the umbrella of *expression*. Feelings associated with the subtlety of motion end up receiving short shrift in most dance classes, even though their expression is expected as proof of talent. The disparity created between *technique* and feelings is symptomatic of seeing mind as prior to body. The mind's great virtue is remembering and organizing. This virtue is the essence of *control*. But the mind is too often out of control, split off from the more subtle, subjective flow of feelings. The underlying expectation is that the dancer will, by virtue of their talent, make the body speak and supersede the mind.

When it came to this sort of technique, I started too late, so I could never catch up, even though I made the cut auditioning for the movie of *West Side Story* with Jerry Robbins, the original choreographer/director, sitting in the orchestra deciding who stays and who goes. My need to satisfy a passion I had arrived at in my early twenties egged me on towards a more embracing way of understanding how feelings come across through movement.

Conceptualizing Teaching

By 1959, after a year at Juilliard, I formulated five requisite elements of dance teaching: *line, form, qualities, space,* and *time*. These elements are built into the syllabus of most techniques. *Line* and *form* are taught through the verticality of the barre work in ballet, and, modern dance techniques, through floor exercises based on short movement phrases from the choreographer's repertoire. Qualities of movement or variations in muscle tonus is also simply imitated. The *space* and *time* elements are taught by following the music.

For those of you who have no idea at all about the differences in these approaches, an analogy of *line* is the *follow-through* in baseball pitching, or batting, or tennis, or in a swimming stroke – a motion that goes all the way through the body, so that arms and legs move fluidly as a whole. I hope this gives you a sense of what I am talking about. Some people obviously have it more naturally; others have to work hard to experience it. *Qualities,* as previously mentioned are variations from tightness to relaxedness of the musculature. This is also taught by *dynamics,* the quickness or slowness by which gestures and shapes vary sequentially. This is true in practically all dance techniques. *Space* and *time* are also taught by imitation and repetitions of directions and musical timing through choreographed movement phrases.

What makes teaching through improvisation distinctive is that each of the elements is explored separately through specific foci, which I either designed or arrived at through trial and error. I discarded whatever I came up with that didn't help the student to experience the specific element totally through their body.

Children

I have earlier mentioned my awakening to creative movement resulting from Jeffrey's *clay* improvisation. It was his very clear *identification* with the smooth and heavy texture of clay that facilitated such a fluid change of shapes without ever losing the *identification.* Regardless of how fast, slow, simple, or complicated his shapes, he maintained the heavy and smooth quality of clay. The faithfulness of his improvising was truly remarkable.

Identification, making something your own, is a developmental phase of childhood that I found worked really well for ages six to eight with the specific images I had formulated. When, I tried it with the five-year-old it did not work, because they had trouble maintaining the unity of form and quality of the images I had worked out. When, I tried it with the nine-year-old, some could still connect to the *images*, but clearly with less intensity, as if they were somehow outside of what's they were doing. Something that allowed for this type of identification had clearly not yet formed with the five-year-old; and that something was no longer fully working with the nine-year-old. The psychological value of *identification* was different for the five-year-old and the nine-year-old. At five they were still focused on their mastery of motion, while at nine they were more self-conscious and involved in this new reflective way with how others saw them. In each stage there is a different body self.

When I tried it with adults, some delighted in the playfulness of *identification,* but never with the same immersion in make-believe. I thought that it would work really well with actors, but once again it varied depending on how meaningfully the actor could access an earlier in life bodily experience. A person's capacity to reawaken an earlier kinetic bodily experience depends on their emotional comfort with regression. The greater the emotional conflicts with the past, the harder it was.

I concluded, through a trial and error approach, that what works and what doesn't depend on finding the particular body focus for each age. Every age connects to the body differently, to a different aspect of the physical experience that brings mind and body together.

Three-year-old appear to experience the body as a *mass* to be released into life with abandon or plopped on the ground like a sack of flour. They would move with total freedom until they would fall down, dizzy with delight. Once the body is in

PRACTICALITY IS HOPE

motion it cannot be stopped quickly. The sensation of motion still holds sway over their tenuous control of movement. The body is *mass* in motion or at rest. The psychological expression of this physical aspect is what makes the three-year old so charming in their growing day-to-day dramas.

Betsy would at times just lay down on the mat and not participate in what the rest of the class was doing. Then she would get up and run with everyone as if nothing had ever happened. You had to accept whatever it was that suddenly took Betsy to lay her body down and whatever it was that made her get up and join the others.

Questions about rhyme or reason do not apply. You have to guess, figure it out. Your instincts with this early age are basic. Feelings come and go physically without the insistence that will become obvious a year later. It seems as though everything is play, although it isn't. Your ability not only to accept but to feel their bodily expression is what makes you a successful teacher with this age group.

Suzy didn't understand when asked, "why are sitting down?" It was as if she were listening to a foreign language. Then she stuck a tight tongue out. Sticking her tongue out, impulsively and unconsciously, as a way of saying *I don't understand, feed me, let me taste it.* Confusing and charming. Three-year-old.

The fours fall in love with the *mastery* of *parts* of the body, as I've mentioned. Strength stands out as they move, run, or freeze their body when the drum stops. *Control is pride.* The negative fours have reached a significant level of obstinacy. They can be tough. Their determination is admirable.

Lilly suddenly surprisingly began to play the piano without any prompting from her parents. Her mother does play.

It's possible to give them assignments about whatever they can think of that moves and suddenly stops. Their improvisations are sometimes delightful.

I am reminded of the difference between three and four moving like a frog. The threes plop when they jump out, the fours maintain body parts they shape like a frog, the fives not only maintain the appearance of body parts but maintain it as they leap; and the sixes hold the shape before and after the leap showing a change in the muscular qualities, from tightness to release to tightness again. This frog example, I hope, gives you a sense of how the relationship to the body changes with age. The reality of the same object registers differently for each age. The object remains the same, the perception of the object's configuration, its muscular movement changes significantly.

I want to credit my ex-wife, Hattie, whose sensitivity to the free spirit of the three and four-year-old resulted in an incredible growth of enrollment, a few years after the initial start of the School. She understood the spirit of their physicality and unconscious impulses as responsive and reactive to her.

Four-year-old Alex told me how much he enjoyed taking a rock and killing the little ants on the ground in his garden. He enjoyed his power, his command over life and death.

Piaget's studies of cognitive development show that the four-year-old can consider something gone forever, while three-year-olds can only imagine that what is missing is somewhere else. Four-year-olds can consider death. Life and death, they can vacillate in extremes. The indelible colors of their personality begin to appear on the palette they will use to paint their character canvasses. Rhythms helped to organize their free spirits in space and movement on the floor, rhythms which they could revert to when their spirits suddenly changed, which could happen in a flash. Balancing walking on the ballet barre while holding their hand or arm or body, as well as tumbling and jumping over the edge of the mat constituted much of the class program. They were excited to explore balance, to challenge their relatively recently acquired control of mobility as the option to show assertiveness.

Mat, three years old, stood at the edge the mat for his first solo flight, "bird in search of food," a story assignment the teacher, Liz Helbraun, gave the group. Before lifting his arms like wings, he stuck his toes out testing the air, as if he were dipping toes into the water, retrieving them quickly into flex knees; then he lifted into an erect body, spreading his wings to sweep into the studio space before bending down to the floor to pick out a worm. His timing was emotionally exquisite. His mother sitting in front of me turned towards me, a tear in both of our eyes, touched by the delicacy of his sense of the bird's motion.

I can say without reservation that Hattie understood their world like the back of her hand, sensed it, felt with them, championed the learning process of impulsivity, its highs and lows.

Imagination, the wellspring of their sensitivity, believing that one is the imagined thing itself, is a basic developmental stage for these toddlers. They imitate spiritually, owning their physicality, which is what their conscious of. They are what they believe they are, like consummate actors, like eighty-five-year-old Bailah telling her family she was having an affair.

I recall having to substitute for Hattie one time with the four-year-olds and being so involved with the "dance class" format of exercise to be followed by creative explorations that I ended up sweating as if I had been rehearsing for an hour without stopping, in my effort to control the class. I didn't know how to follow their lead, to engage learning by picking up on the physical expressions of their emotional urges, emotional expressions they weren't necessarily conscious of. It is startling now as a psychoanalyst to realize how out of touch I was with feelings expressed through impulses. And how the sense of order (form) had become so powerfully central to my understanding. I had no idea how much *control of motion external and internal* meant to their burgeoning sense of independence. The exploratory physical self-learning about *control* was shifting to *fixations,* preferred activities they had learned to control representing what they feel. "I want you to, see what I want to show you," an insistence that implied a relentless NO to any alternative activity. A stage of growth many never give up as the bottom line, as if their individuality would collapse into a swarm of mind flies buzzing around. For them, anxiety was replacing fear. Body and soul, the twins of spirit parting like strangers in the night. I had much to learn in the years to follow.

To my engineering logical mind, *parts* of the body needed to be coordinated into *line*. The line that grows out of the single dot, a continuous uninterrupted line. It was this kind of thinking that led to considering locomotion as line. I thought of sliding as line, of turning as line, a step by step walk as line, jumping as a jerky line. All other locomotion are permutations or combinations of these basic four. Twisting is part of turning, hopping is part of jumping, and so on. To help the five-year-old to engage this locomotion throughout the body I showed the parts that can move without moving another part. I showed sliding with the hand, followed by sliding with the elbow, followed by sliding with the shoulder, then the whole arm.

We explored twenty-three *parts* of the body that can move independently without moving any other part:

> fingers (2), hands (2), elbows (2), shoulders (2), arms (2), head (1), torso-rib cage (1), whole torso (1), hip (1), legs (2) knees (2), foot (2), toes (2), whole body (1).

This skeletal definition combined with a controllable specific intent, delighted the fives. It was an idea I came up with to creatively teach *line* that worked. They enjoyed playing with these explorations beyond my wildest expectations. They would slide from one part to another until they became a *sliding thing*.

Jennifer became a snake; Suzy became flowing water; Margaret became finger painting on paper.

They easily internalized the motion of what they were doing on the outside into an internal imaged experience, an association with a body. *The motion of* movement was still their medium for *identifying*. However, *identification* was becoming more distinguished, sliding is a more abstract and distinct sort of thing, as an aspect of action, and more conceptual than being a bird.

This brings to mind stopping at the end of a class to sit for a while and talk about their favorite *locomotion*. There were always a couple of girls who would quickly come to sit very close to me as if I was manna from heaven for their unconscious emotional life of love, of freedom. Their imagination was becoming defined. "I want to be a ballerina. I want to be a nurse. I want to be..." came leaping out of their mouths like a cornucopia of flowers and ripe fruit. There were a few years when I couldn't wait for the five-year-old class on Friday. They made me love them. They could motorize an imaginative self and cast it into the future – a motorized sensory continuous expression of self. Each child had a favorite *locomotion* expressive of how they thought of their self-assertion. If the child was more impulsive becoming a *jumping thing* was their favorite, expressing the suddenness with which they experience their feelings. If the child is more calculating than *walking* is their favorite. *Turning* is for the child that experiences feelings without inhibition, like a three-year old; and *sliding* the most commonly liked of the locomotion, followed by *jumping,* is for the child that doesn't like being ruffled. This is an expression of what will be abstracted in dance parlance as *line*. Each age expresses their feelings through different way of sensing the body. This understanding shaped my creative movement curriculum for each age.

Just as *form/effort* became the exploratory determinant for the six to eight-year-olds, (see my book, *Creative Movement for Children: A Dance Program for the Classroom*), my schema of the elements that constitute all dance training follows *form* and *qualities.* The nine and ten-year-old unquestionably enter life in *space*. Social relationships and cliques are serious business for them. Their self-consciousness is heightened by peer relationships. They don't just lie down for a little bit when they feel low, like three-year-old, they sulk. Emotions wash over them like a downpour. In the "olden days" no child under the age of nine would ever be taken to a ballet class, because the bones don't fully harden until they are nine. But there is another reason, because of their self-consciousness they are ready to follow defined instructions. I recall my daughters' friends at that age. Each of them had somehow developed some peculiar control of their finger joints or a special face contortion that set them apart from each other. Identity was becoming a conscious aspect of their growing up. Claiming and demonstrating control of their hands and face expressed how distinctively they could harness their competitive energy. This affected their exercise syllabus in our dance classes, but it made the improvisational work problematic. The notion that they could explore *space* as an independent framework just didn't work. They're okay if you give them actions, things to follow, imitate, control, but they are not ready to explore individually through improvisation. That is why gymnastics and ballet begin to fit into their psychological make-up. Unfortunately, and unwittingly they are diminishing their connection to an earlier fantasy life, an earlier way of experiencing the impact of the stimuli around and within them.

Both Gwen Vernon and Rita Moreno brought their daughters into the creative movement class, leery of the rigidity inherent in the ballet discipline. They wanted their daughters to first experience dance as free improvisations of their souls. They knew full well their own learning experience, which they had learned to overcome in order to tap into their own creative potential. I was honored by two Broadway stars' appreciation of creative movement. Reminding me of renowned soloist musicians who also valued the creative movement experience for their children, the musicians Pinchas and Eugenia Zuckerman, Peter Serkin, plus Michael Gilbert and Yoko Takabe, violinists of the New York Philharmonic, parents of Jennifer and Alan. Alan as I have earlier noted would become the conductor of the New York Philharmonic some years later. Memories of so many of the liberal democrats of the Upper West Side of New York, and children of psychoanalysts on the West Side of Manhattan.

Along with this social aspect of nine and ten-year-old is the physical transformations they are experiencing, silently, looking around at their peers, comparing internally, not necessarily with each other. They begin to be complicated in a new way because they stand at the cusp of transitioning into adolescence. The transformations that seem so relatively gentle at nine and ten become exponentially sharper in each ensuing year.

Lyn Pyle, the second teacher I hired, as enrollment at The School for Creative Movement (SCM) grew, arrived with a master's degree in comparative literature from Berkley. She was training at The Henry Street Settlement with Alwin Nikolais and Murray Lewis, who were exploring *form and space* choreographically, elements that had already become central to my thinking.

The strong socio-political sensibility that was already a part of her character made her responsive to the needs of the nine and ten-year-old. In discussing the problems with those age groups, improvisational freedom or lack of it, Lyn came up with a terrific idea – sheets. They can continue to explore *clay, wire, rubber band* and *piano,* specific images for exploring *qualities* and *form* under the sheets. The sheets protected them from judgmental eyes. Judgments that had more to do with their own self-consciousness than with what other people, peers or teachers, were thinking. They were covering up their own developing separation and potential self and sexual assertiveness from family, their own guilt about leaving the nest, with varying degrees of shame for their burgeoning desires as nature kept tapping at the door of their innocence.

It was titillating to look at shapes under the sheets, to see the hardness of *wire* changing the shapes of the sheets, or the elasticity of *rubber band* shapes affecting the landscape of the sheets like rolling hills. It was gratifying to witness the power of their individuality coming through despite the defensive cover of the sheets. I remain grateful to Lyn for finding a creative movement solution for the problems of subconscious guilt and unconscious shame that manifests in using *space* in a subjective improvisation that is the essence of Creative Movement. Overcoming inhibition, shyness, shame, or guilt, often driven by even more primitive aggressive fears, is difficult. *Sheets* was a brainstorm idea. Lyn who was also part of a newly formed street theater co-op understood reaching out as fundamental in social settings. She went on after many years heading Mass Transit Theater to form a mediation program for a number of New York Board of Education Schools affecting how violence can be handled cooperatively and effectively by peers. I am honored by her continuing to take classes with me, honoring fifty plus years of working together.

The eleven through thirteen group began to show more readiness for physical and thus emotional exposure. Since this more exhibitionistic readiness varies, we continued to use the sheets: with the option of using the sheets as cover, revealing as much or as little of themselves as they feel prepared to do, or tearing the sheet off to wrap it around themselves like a cape or discard it on the floor. A more complicated option developed which was to exchange sheets or use them for gathering together.

Commentary

Since these options give greater license for aggressive and self-assertive movement, the *sense of form* explored with the six to eight-year-olds, followed by the sheets with the nine to eleven age group, begins to be compromised by virtue of the self-assertive impulses with the twelve to fourteen age group, reminding me of the potential wildness of the two-year-old. Their biological changes make unconscious and conscious demands as the child is threatened by how their body is altering. A more internal sense of "togetherness" needed to be found.

The *identification foci* (what Winnicott would call "transitional objects") of locomotion, images, or sheets were wearing thin as the children got older. Substitute stories, images, and objects were becoming more abstract, not felt in the body as they had been at earlier ages. Improvisational movement creativity had to be approached more directly.

Psychotherapeutic perspectives may treat the expression of the aggressive drive as an inner force towards autonomy, as a positive act of "separation/individuation." From a dance perspective, as the boundaries of cohesion give way to dramatic and demonstrative gestures (often isolated from the whole of the body) symptomatic of psychological *splitting*, a creative solution is screaming for attention. Exhibitionism, impulsiveness, and intuitions need to be integrated. Attitudes, opinions, impulses are being treated by this adolescent age group as feelings. They are daring and courageous, sharpening their maturing character.

I have come to understand that the freedom of impulses (what most people think of as "gut feelings"), even within a creative artistic framework, serves to mask the subtle flow of feelings on a much deeper level of self-experience. Impulses are feelings that have been somaticized (I'll have more to say about this later.)

In my work with them as they age, the children's exercises become more specific and increasingly more technical, combining floor and barre work. The barre work for fourteen through sixteen-year-olds is quite balletic, with an emphasis on *motion through muscles*. A great deal of attention was paid to each individual's perceptual sensitivity – how clearly does each individual sense the sensation of motion through the muscles. In this, my approach diverged from the balletic positions at the barre and positioned figures in modern dance techniques.

I am reminded that a sense of motion through muscles was useless before the age of seven and a half to eight, when they can distinguish muscular contraction and extensions consciously. It was this development of muscular sensitivity that made the image of the rubber *band* creatively meaningful. Sensitivity to motion through the musculature depends on enough muscular development to sense motion *tactilely*. At earlier ages the body is an *object* filled or hollow, imagined as a seed, a flower, a sliding thing, a piece of clay. It may be marvelous or frightening. Some people remain trapped in an imagined body. It is hard to convince an anorexic that they are too thin – a dramatic example of an imagined body.

The freer creative movement explorations for this older group dealt with *directions in space*. There are nine directions: 1/ forward, 2/ backward, 3/ sideways, 4/ diagonals, 5/ down, 6/ up, 7/ in, 8/ out, 9/ around. To ensure they were sensing the directions bodily, I would ask them to move forward by sensing the front of their body, their face, then the throat, the upper chest, the rib cage, the abdominal part of the torso, and so on down to the toes. It was a visual, imagined progression but it also enlisted their physical perception of the musculature. They would walk around the studio continually focusing on the front of the body until they could run without losing the sense of the front of the body, at which point I would introduce music for them to improvise, while never losing sensing the front of their body. We would do this with every direction. As with the exploration of motion with adults, it helped to ensure a more physical subjective experience moving in space. This was in keeping with what happens in both ballet and modern dance, with the across the floor spatial training that focuses on the external instruction, but it included the emphasis on the internal sensibility coming through. It would take quite a number of classes to reinforce their *kinesthetic sense of self.*

Cultivating the ability to continually image the direction physically was part of my effort to develop a sense of *form* by sensing the surfaces of form. All forms have a front, back, top, bottom, and inner and outer aspect that constitutes the whole. In retrospect, it was an approach to sensitizing imaging. It was comparable to many of the Stanislavsky theater techniques used by actors, like Marlon Brando, James Dean and Montgomery Cliff, who came out of the Actors Studio, where they were taught to tap into their sensory experiences.

This brings to mind a composition class with Lucas Hoving (who was a principal dancer with Jose Limon's company) who spoke about space as *filled or empty.* If filled, one's movement had to push through space, carve it with one's gestures and figures; if empty, one drew lines in space, like a Saul Steinberg line drawing from *The New Yorker* magazine. *Filled* or *empty* space is an imagined projection, to elicit in the performer a qualitative sense of self engaging the surround of space. It is in essence a way to make the person aware of their muscular effort. On a psychological level, *filled space* is an experience of life and people as resistances that have to be overcome. *Empty space* is the opposite, at least with people who feel a strong sense of self-confidence. On a muscular level, *filled or empty* breaks down as muscle tonus, the quality of muscle tension colored by a person's emotional sense of social and personal freedom. Marcel Marceau, the French pantomimist, always showed the *effort* of the gesture in all of his miming. When he was 'opening a curtain,' you could feel its weight. His focus was on how, in order to live, we have to exert effort. In contrast, in the style of Jean Louis Barrault (another French pantomimist) 'parting the curtain' would be a simple and effortless gesture; it was as if he was parting feathers. Barrault's gestural style was like the earlier Japanese Noh theater that predates Kabuki. Barrault focused on the symbolic act of passing from one place to enter another place. A timeless gesture. Filled or empty comes down to the muscular effort of a gesture, and the effort breaks down to how a person senses their body to communicate what they feel.

How available is our body?

This direct conscious approach to imaging *sensation*, rather than *identification*, would continue to dictate my approach with adults. Exploring the *memory of sensation* was replacing *identification with* an object. *Space*, how one senses and uses it, took on a sensory dimension rather than the more common logical focus on intention, i.e., the purpose for crossing this space. Focusing on intention and motivation puts the emphasis on action and attitudes taken about the action. This requires subordinating the bodily sensation. If both the kinetic and the kinesthetic stay alive consciously, art happens.

Sometime after, I found following "directions" a limited and not very creative approach.

Sensations about purpose and actions do not generate an internal bodily and spatial experience. They heighten sensitivity for what is being controlled, but do not evoke the inner voice that identifications did. I had to find something else.

In an effort to try more evocative and generating foci, I recalled my experience with Aryeh Kalev, an Israeli man with a burgeoning dance school in a suburb of Tel Aviv. Years later he and his eldest daughter attended one of my two-week summer Teacher Training workshops. We first met in 1957, when we shared a room at the American Dance Festival summer program. He came to the U.S. for six months with a scholarship from the Martha Graham school. He was originally from Czechoslovakia, the son of a big department store family. He was saved from the Nazi invasion by the Zionist initiative Youth Aliya, organized to take children out of endangered countries to Israel. The children were usually settled in one of a number of collective settlements that were committed to the rescue of these children. He developed athletically, and the kibbutz sponsored his education in gymnastics in Switzerland. His physical interest also included yoga. He was older, and clearly more mature emotionally, than I was at the time. He was a quiet and very observant man.

One late morning returning to our room after a couple of morning technique classes, I must have been bothered by something and probably began to grumble in Hebrew to Aryeh.

He listened and was moved to ask me if I wanted to try a relaxation technique that he had learned. I said Yes. He pulled an army blanket off the bed, doubled it over, and laid it out on the floor, and had me lie down on it on my back. He adjusted my head by centering it both horizontally and vertically, asking me to note exactly the point upon which my head lay. He asked me to place my legs equidistant from the center of my body, and my arms, palms down, flat on the blanket, equidistant from my thighs. We did all this very slowly and very quietly. He sat on the bed talking me through the steps.

"Close your eyes." He waited. "Sense the spot on the back of your head touching the blanket." He waited. "Imagine the spot as the center, as if it is the spot where the thrown stone falls into a pool of water, where the water moves outward in circles. Tilt your head a very little bit to your left, and then back to the center." I did. "Please, do the same to the right." I did. "Please, repeat, left and right, on your own a few times, always being able to return to the center." I did. I realized how unconsciously I had thought the center of my head more to the right of the centering spot he had placed it. My new center felt strange, although I made sure not to change it. "From the center point of the head draw a line down your neck very slowly, then continue into the right shoulder."

He waited to see the motion happening through the neck and into the shoulder, then said, 'down the upper arm through the elbow." Once again, waiting. I began to feel impatience with how long it was taking him to speak these directions, one step at a time, in one series after another, the ends of which I already knew.

"Now through the forearm into the wrist." I waited and began to sense the line I was drawing more definitively. "Let the line go into the tip of your thumb." This deliberately slow instructive process continued through the rest of the fingers. The line became clearer and clearer. "Please, return to the center of your head, make sure to sense the same spot." He continued, asking me to draw a line down the left arm to the tips of the fingers, with the same measured voice that never became monotonic. Following this visibly tempered approach, I drew down the right side of my torso into the tips of my right toes, repeating the same process on my left side. I had lost the sense of time.

"Just breathe in and breathe out. Sense the inhalation going through your head and down your back. Sense the exhalation rising from the stomach and out your mouth." After a number inhalation and exhalations, my chest began to heave like I was sobbing, tearless sobs. It shocked me, but I didn't interrupt the process I had committed to. My chest relaxed into a quiet in-and-out breathing. Finally, I had relaxed, with no sense of trying to relax. The simple process of breathing was all that was happening. Then he suggested that we should stop to go to lunch. He asked me how I was feeling. I said I was fine, looked at my watch and saw that lunch had already started. I had quickly reverted to my normal attitude, as if what I had just gone through was interesting but not life-changing or character altering.

We walked out onto the path to the cafeteria. I was suddenly experiencing a lightness, almost like floating, hardly feeling my feet on the ground. My steps felt shockingly light. I also experienced the architectural design of the inner campus spaces, seeing that space was as much a part of the composition of the campus as the buildings. An awareness of self in space was coming into my felt awareness. The sheer lightness of my steps was my strongest sense as we entered the building, took our lunch, and sat down. The sensation of lightness lasted for several hours, slowly shifting from an experience into a memory.

It was this centering experience that came to mind as I was searching for a creative approach to explore space. It reminded me of the evocativeness of Jeffrey's clay improvisation. Something inside was accompanying the outside actions.

When the oldest 14-15 all-girls class formed, I took them through a shortened version of the routine Aryeh had shown me. When they stood up, I could see their arms hanging lower, as if they had stretched. I asked how their arms felt. Each of them told me that they felt longer. I asked about other parts of the body that seemed different to me, maintaining the same innocence of voice so as not to suggest that I knew. I was, by the middle to late 1960s, extremely conscious of the power of suggestion. I proceeded carefully. Since I was doing this for the sake of seeing if their sense of space was affected internally. I asked them to improvise. I believe I asked them to improvise with whatever they were sensing. They started by laying on the floor. One of the girls imagined herself as a snake slithering on the ground, magically sprouting wings, rising into flight. A mythical enactment. The other girls had comparable experiences, albeit more literal, not as mythic. I felt that I had found a creative teaching approach to *space explorations* – New Centers.

My creative movement discoveries were unwittingly getting me out of my unconsciously committed aloneness, out of persistent physical tension, out of living in the throes of anxiety.

The full-fledged program for children lasted from 1962-1980 on the Upper West Side of Manhattan. A more abbreviated program for preschoolers and ages six and seven continued, when the School moved to the Chelsea area of Manhattan. The neighborhood clientele established over the first eighteen years of what was the only creative modern dance school on the West Side would never reemerge in the Chelsea area. Life had changed; this is when gymnastics became popular through the Olympics. Also, the creative atmosphere of the sixties and early seventies *zeitgeist* had changed. The children's program lasted in the Chelsea area from 1980-1992. Thereafter, I returned to the upper West Side to teach only adults, and to my psychotherapy and psychoanalytic practice.

Adults

I quickly discovered that adults needed a different gateway to enter the body. Adults may still identify, but not as wholeheartedly as children. They can imitate but don't experience their imitation in the transformative way children do. Adults demand restraints, because they can in fact do all the things that children could only imagine doing.

As a neighborhood school, it drew adults mostly from the area, although occasionally a quasi-professional dancer interested in creative movement would appear. It became obvious that following movement phrases across the diagonal of the studio, the longest line of the space, standard in professional classes, met with some confusion. They would, seemingly without realizing it, forget the placement or movement of an arm, or get frustrated by a misstep. Although they understood the professional format, they have developed too much individuality, interests that were not whole-body, physically focused. Although I quickly managed to breakdown the combination of steps and upper body movement into their simplest walking, one-two-three, and so on, steps, the transmission from observation and memory to kinetics, let alone kinesthetic, was not easy.

A movement phrase is a combination of steps in one or several directions, combining upper body movement and gestures to either eight or sixteen measures of music. The steps, and movements are considered *mechanics*. Sharp changes or sudden stops in the flow of the combination of movements is considered *dynamics*, usually dictated by rhythms. The overall character of mechanics and dynamics is the spirit of the phrase.

Just describing a movement phrase, while recalling some of the people in my adult classes, brings up a sense of frustration. Even though the movement phrase may be simple from a dancer's point of view, my expectation was that the adult students would follow the demonstrated movement. Not only is this standard dance class procedure, it is a quick way to eliminate people in professional auditions, where a phrase of sixteen counts is shown once or twice and followed immediately by a "Thank you," indicating the rejection of someone who could not follow.

Imitation is basic. We all learn the basics of being a self from early in life through imitation. In professional auditions and rehearsals, the limitations of time are severe, changes are constantly being made at the last moment, and there is no time to teach. Quick imitation, being ready to copy immediately is essential. If the dancer is able to absorb the essential character of the choreographer's intention, so much the better, but performing the demonstrated steps and dynamics is basic.

Fundamentally, it is always about testing how sensitively the dancer is sensing the spirit of the choreography.

Adults coming to a creative movement dance class are expecting a more personally crafted individual experience. I would characterize the adult enrolling students as excited and wishing to move. The range of their expectations and motivations is very wide, so the ability of the teacher to relate, to sense the specifics of their underlying "excitement and wish" is important. That capacity, that wish to relate is what made my work with children so successful, and it also helped the adult classes develop. In response to the difficulties that arose, I would deconstruct the phrase into 1) Step right with right foot, 2) Left leg crosses behind, and 3) Step right with right leg, and so on, with the swing of the arms. The explanation seems simple enough but having to repeat that instruction a few times so that everyone gets it ends up being arduous and at times, oddly, confusing for students who pick up on the physicality of the combination. The students who were so quick on the uptake were often found when I was breaking it down confusing.

I have mentioned a woman who had this natural capacity to imitate the focal sense of a physical demonstration, but for whom breaking the foci down to the tactile muscular process was a death knoll.

This same distinction is found in psychotherapy when a patient grasps emotionally what is being conveyed but finds the explanation or interpretation an incomprehensible jumble of words.

Breaking it down to the actual activity of the muscles has the effect of destroying the wholeness of the object and the ability to perform the activity that had been unconsciously absorbed. It takes all the fun out of the motion of dance. It's a sure way to lose business.

Beginner's Level

I quickly shifted to a generalized sequence– step right with a swing of the arm, then, left with a swing of the other arm. I refocused on the freedom of movement, the thrust of the body, reminiscent of three-year-old. I wasn't thinking of feelings, but intuitively activating the thrill of movement, the inherent aggression of movement. Seeing the smile on my adult student's faces, and my not being judgmental, told me that I was on the right track. We were playing, letting them feel the pleasure, reinforcing what most of us experience early in life when we stand, run, turn, and change direction at will.

I always used a variety of music with every inventive focus that, in retrospect, was getting the adults to thrust – slower, softer, harder, teaching *dynamics*, what I called *qualities* (changes in muscle tonus). This approach never undermined the freedom/delight of movement.

I was very sensitive to tension in the body. How could I open their breathing? Breathing changes as we go from walking to running. Every change in *effort* alters our breathing. And, in fact, even the slightest shift in feelings alters the breath. Feelings autonomically alter muscular tonus (or the tension in muscles) with an immediacy that easily by-passes our consciousness. It is this connection of the breath to change that has made the breath so basic for meditation and relaxation practices. But how do I engage the breathing in improvisation while moving?

I used varying pieces of music, each piece with a different tempo, a different *feeling/breathing* time. I asked the students to run around the studio with an awareness of how their breathing was changing as they were running while trying to accommodate the tempo of the music, then to keep on running until they sensed the running, the breath, and the music falling into sync. Some people got it quickly, others tended to do what they usually did with music, namely: connect to the phrasing and a rhythm they are comfortable with. Usually emphasizing the first note as a downbeat and swaying the body into the third beat of the measure, which doesn't alter their habitual breathing pattern, which functions as an unconscious emotional fixation. Not altering their breathing is a way to unconsciously control their emotional sense of self. It is an accommodation to a relationship, without being affected to experience the tempo of the music, that is never entering into the feeling of the music, the composer's feeling. It became necessary to demonstrate the difference between phrasing and running to the tempo. Once they saw the difference, they were able to sync running, breathing and music. They were still understanding by imitating me through my demonstration. From my present psychoanalytic perspective, they were unconsciously holding on to the relationship to me. They were not entering into their own internal sense of feelings.

Once they sensed the "sync" they could continue moving or stand still, because the tempo was sustained internally. It promoted their sensory connection to the spirit of the music, physically. We all naturally make relational connections on an unconscious level. We also manifest rejection and conflicts of relationship, especially early in life, muscularly on an unconscious level. Consequently, the explorations with breathing and "syncing" breath, body, and music were unconsciously loosening their somaticized tensions without their having to verbally analyze the nature of their emotional fixations. Improvisational possibilities were being opened – tension released. I was inadvertently doing movement therapy by teaching the freedom of dance.

All psychological holding in the body is based on fear and self-protection and centered in the basic demand for safety. Breathing patterns can be thought of from this perspective. Breathing practices have been employed for thousands of years. Humans connected breath with attitude a long time ago. Somaticized emotional defenses were being affected in the dance class through the assertiveness of movement, rather than through the physical stillness of meditation or talk therapy.

I want to stress that insights in therapy do release physical tensions. Meditation can also have this effect. But neither change misalignments. And our misalignments are the somatic basis of habits.

Inherent in the process of releasing through opening up breathing patterns is the awareness of the flow of motion. I explored the *element* of *motion* by having the students run in a circle, arms extended at shoulder height, slowly bending the torso towards the middle of the circle, with eyes looking at the center on the floor of the circle. This visual focus towards the center of the circle while maintaining the circle by running as a group induces the sensation of motion hypnotically, very much like a ritual. I came to realize that this approach mimics how bodily experience becomes memory – sensations become memory. Feelings come and go, sensations are remembered.

I would then ask them while continuing to move to imagine the sensation of motion moving through their body – their arms, torso, neck, pelvis, and so on – without stopping. I continued this exploration and ensuring the awareness of breath of motion with a variety of music.

This sense of motion is intrinsic to dancers and musicians, helping to ensure their internal sense of one of the elements of dance. These were techniques I developed to have them experience the physical elements of dancing rather than merely imagining them.

The next element to be explored was *beat*. Using a piece of music with a strong beat, I would have them stand in place stomping feet one, one, one, on the beat. I would demonstrate how to do this. For a lot of people, as odd as that may seem, it was not clear what it meant to *stomp to the beat*. Some people live on such an internal level, a fantasy, if you will, that the reality of a beat doesn't automatically register. They judge the beat and protect themselves emotionally, if the beat is too demanding, and thus unconsciously reminiscent of conflicts with demands early in their lives. This was also done in a circle, that made it easier for people to follow. Circles unify, folk dances are a clear demonstration of this. Once again, when everyone was on the beat, I would ask them to continue the beat standing in place. Then continue moving to keep the beat with the knees while continuing to stomp the feet. Then shift to sustain the beat with just knees, then just hips, then just torso, then just arms, then just hands, then fingers, then thumb, then just tongue, and then stop all movement to realize that the beat was sustained by memory.

It became clear to everyone that **beat is memory**. Beat helps to organize, to control, creating a sense of unity. It is that unity that induces a sense of safety and of togetherness.

We explored beat with a variety of music, from Dave Brubeck to Vivaldi. They could hear the beat as a distinct organization of sound differentiated from the phrasing. Phrasing is usually organized by a downbeat accent on the first note of a measure, which people usually are comfortable with, they "get it" unconsciously. To reinforce their sense of beat, I would ask them to step on the first beat while not moving on the next three beats. Once they were able to sense the beat, they had the option to dance with it in whatever ways they wanted it to come through their improvisation.

The process of internalizing what was explored externally liberated their options for their own creative movement.

Every element was explored over a period of weeks, until I sensed that everyone got it. It was then combined with the next element. Breath, with and without motion; motion combined with and without breath; and beat combined with and without breath or motion. This process of distinguishing proved to them the value of these elements in gaining a fuller and more meaningful experience of movement. It helped them to sense their sensations more consciously, while simultaneously relaxing their control and their musculature.

Breath, motion, and beat: these three elements constituted the curriculum for beginners coming once a week for an hour class for three sixteen-week sessions per year for two years. This conscious approach to internalizing these basic elements made imitation easier and less conflictual. It created a more independent body, less governed by unexamined habit and judgments. It got us away from the "some people have it, and some people don't" mentality. We all have it. This was proven by a constant growth of enrollment and students continuing from year to year telling me by their commitment that they were enjoying the experience of the process.

Intermediate Level

Preparing the beginner level students to integrate the fundamentals of breathing, motion and beat into their physicality facilitated their moving out of their own impulses and intuitions. Consequently, *gestures* and *shapes* that give form to their impulses, their intuitions, became the next hurdle to finding a creative teaching approach to generate their feelings.

I approached the exploration of *gesture* by focusing on an awareness of the part of the body they move – a hand, an arm, whatever. I was now engaging the body proper, what is actually moving, **using** the body as an expression of the pleasure of freedom.

The freedom of movement was solidly established through the explorations of **breath** as a physical awareness to liberate choice, **motion** to facilitate the spatial freedom of fantasy, and **beat** to validate memory as the organization of choice. These are all essentially psychologically driven explorations using the body as the grounding for these freedoms.

Gesture is an acknowledgement of the body. Gesture is a literal awareness of physical assertiveness.

I initiated this awareness by asking them to treat each breath as a *gesture*. The self-consciousness of this act surprised them. Standing still and treating the inhalation as a *gesture*, as well as the exhalation as a *gesture*, effectively brought a consciousness of what the body is doing as it functions in the present moment. Some people found this level of awareness annoying, as if questioning their choiceless bodily habits. I now understand it as not wanting to reawaken physiologic experiences tied to negative associations. *(See chapter on what gets reversed).*

Continuing in this self-conscious vein, the motion of the leg to take a step is a *gesture*. This inhibiting consciousness disappears as the person moves from *gesture to gesture* walking, to, finally, moving to music. This exploration heightened the awareness of *motion*, enhancing a sensitivity to actions. The usual consideration of *gestures* as subordinate to the purpose of the *gesture* was being made more conscious and thus qualitatively more meaningful. The subjective experience of *gesture* was heightened, its effects on others became more obvious. Intention, execution, and implication were being brought together.

I certainly felt more conscious and convinced myself that the body and the body's movements were becoming more real for the students. This was an effort on my part to treat the body as more than just an instrument for control and gratification of wishes and aims. It was making conscious the body itself as expression. One can think of this as analogous to the painter's awareness of the brush stroke, or the pianist's awareness of the finger striking the key, or a carpenter's awareness of the stroke of the plane on the wood he is shaving. It diminishes the self-righteousness of intention by heightening the "how" and the "what" of the intent.

Form is the container of *gestures*. However, the consciousness of *form* doesn't automatically enlist the consciousness of *gesture*, which, as I've mentioned, is often overshadowed by our self-justifying sense of purpose. The return to *form, of its bodily actuality* reawakened the problems that initiated the *breath* explorations. It was too much physicality to be conscious of – that is, too much when the body is essentially an instrument of wishes, of desires, of the mind.

To actualize the sense of *form*, I began to explore *directions*, in the same way as I had done with the older girls' class – sense the front of the face as they move into space, then the chest, then the pelvis, until they could sense the whole *front* of the body as they moved forward. This seemed to work more effectively to build the sense of *form* rather than leaving them merely imagining *gestures*.

Form still remained for me the core sensibility of professional training. I did the same for the *back* as for the *front*. Sense the back of the head, the neck and so on, down the body. Each time a plane of the body was explored it was then combined with the next plane, thus slowly building the elements that comprise a solid imagining of the whole body as *form*. Inherent in front, back, sides and diagonals are a two-dimensional, horizontal plane of space; while *up* and *down*, adds a vertical, three-dimensional plane, then *in* and *out* creates a sense of the body as volume, a fourth dimension. This continued by combining various dimensions making the wished-for *form* more real for the adult students. You can think of these directional explorations as a sensory awakening to the planes of the body – sensory experience that feeds memory. Once the body as *form* is made conscious, the awareness of an outside and an inside becomes tangible. The totally intentional sense of the body was being filled out by these physical explorations.

These explorations were always accompanied by music that associatively paralleled each one of the directions, to stimulate improvisation. As with the five-year-old, each person discovered which of the *directions* held more meaning for them, eliciting repressed unconscious feelings associated with that plane. Although we never addressed these possible associations verbally, they were sometimes simply shared by the student. I would also reinforce, out of my own experience, the emotional significance of each *direction* by demonstrating the difference in theatrical styles: Commedia as primarily driven by *front*, as are most musicals, considered as presentational, towards the audience, like Shakespearian asides; Ibsen or O'Neill as mostly *back,* representational; Strindberg, Dostoyevsky as mostly *in,* grabbling with the internal conflicts; Restoration drama as mostly *up,* quick overlapping dialogues, social, cocktail party banter; Classic Greek theater as *in and down,* awaiting fate. Pantomimic classic ballet was significantly altered by Balanchine's fluidity showing the emotional *inner* high of the freedom of movement, or Tudor's psychologically driven ballets that were even more *internal,* closer to Strindberg's plays. Grahams gestural symbolism took the *in and down* of emotions into *in as out.* Thus, *directions* became more than just spatial. *Directions* are emotionally charged psychosocial expressions of the self. They became a physical technique for theatrical styles for actors' movement training, exploring the physical and emotionally laden plasticity, so obvious in the silent movies of Chaplin, Keaton, or Laurence Olivier in *The Entertainer,* or the subtlety of Anthony Hopkins in *The Remains of the Day.*

What became clearer to me was how much the body for adults is a spatial object that made the *directions* exploration so effective. The body as a social reality in space, that I noted for girls at nine has come into full bloom for most adults. The body of sensations apparent with the threes, subsumed by aims and wishes was being brought into emotional awareness by the exploration of *form*.

Although the sense of *form* was significantly heightened by these explorations, the improvisational movement language remained circumscribed, uninteresting. It reminded me of the seven-year old boys' improvisations on what they thought of as heavy that were imitative, without truly sensing the inner core of what they were imitating.

In the hope of trying to evoke a more inner level of physical aliveness, I demonstrated vibrating *impulses* within *gestures*. I was asking them to be sensitive to possible enervations: a trembling within the musculature of the arm as it is extended, or a sudden twist as the torso moved forward, an unexpected change in the internal life of any action, or of a gesture, or a change of form or direction.

In retrospect, I was asking them through these physical explorations to be alive to inner doubt, to the uncertainty of ambivalence, to unconscious *reversals*, and denial, to holding back muscularly, to the power of fear.

It would appear liberating, but it wasn't. The adult's psychophysical defenses had become too strong, too fixed. There were some individuals for whom this notion of *impulses* facilitated a more subjective movement language but, by and large, its effectiveness was short lived. The psychological mechanisms that shut us down are powerful. It was the effort to understand and describe this shutting down mechanism that started psychoanalysis.

What remained salient was their tendency to create a "relationship" to the music. A relationship to music is a socializing. If you think of the music as the voice of another, a substitute for a person, then instinctively our tendency is to relate. From a psychoanalytic perspective, the immediacy of relating to the music is an automatic unconscious *transference*. Relating to prerecorded music, to an unchanging Other to whom we must make all the accommodations, like when we were infants, because it/they – cannot. Needless to say, this immediate effort to interact with the music is common, although, some people seem unable to move to music; they will not leave themselves or lose themselves in it. Whatever they have built up as self-protective is inviolate.

Is the immediacy with which we so readily submit to the music a resistance? Is it a defense against the awareness of the motion moving through our muscles? Is this a psychophysical unconscious defense against feelings? Does this tendency impact on a more personal movement language, given that most people accommodate the organizational phrasing of the music, the rhythmic structure, the downbeat of the music? In fact, it is usually boredom or the wish to assert a more individual voice that prompts movement inventions. Inventions are intuitive constructions, a clever moment in time, like disco dancing. These inventions carry the kernel of feeling but are quickly covered up by the repetition of the invented gesture sealing the kernel of feelings.

Why does the more personal sense of *form*, of *gesture*, of *impulses* so readily get absorbed into and assimilated to the music, to the Other? These questions became central to my thoughts about creative movement, my psychoanalytic sensibilities heightened my awareness.

In a continuing effort to have them become more sensitive to what is moving around inside of the gesture – the form, impulses, and intuition – I suggested they try to move with a sense of their body's weight, a sense of their body as mass. We explored *weight with the breath, with motion, with beat.* This made for a more distinct physicality. As I have already mentioned, one person did have a violent reaction because of her personal unconscious association to weight. She related to weight as literal and didn't grasp my contextual intent. The request that they sense the weight of the body encouraged the use of the floor in their improvisations, naturally, extending their spatial environment, enhancing their subjective experience.

The sense of weight began to elicit a more subjective engagement. It wasn't as connected or free as I had hoped, however, staying in the body took on gravitas. It became obvious that *weight* needs to be channeled, if it is not to just drop as the woman who shouted at me, "why do you want us to die?" The channel became obvious – **muscles.** Our mind can, and at times does make an image, a metaphor concrete, literal, showing us the absurdity of poetry when the context is not clear.

Advanced Level – Space

It began by recalling the concentration exercise mentioned earlier for a small group of 14 -15-year-olds. These explorations as will be clearer were my creative movement approach to exploring *space.*

The time for the *concentration exercises* demanded extending the class to one and a half hours. They would lie on their backs as I talked them through this imagined line descending through the body from the *back center of the head.* Then getting up slowly sustaining the focus on the *back center of the head* to walk and subsequently improvise to music.

The Center became a fixed point from which gestures emanated so that arms felt longer, and legs felt far away. The shift in their sensory experience from their usual sense of their body was, if nothing else, engaging. Sensation became – or, reverted to being, once again – a fundamentally interesting experience for the mind. Their responsiveness to the *back of the head center* led to exploring *the front head center* with the same visualization of lines to the tips of the fingers and toes. The *front head center* combined *direction with the center*. It was interesting to note that the *center* remained a stronger focus than the *direction* pointing to the internal focus as more fixating than the directive foci of intention.

This was followed by the *middle head center* accentuating the *head center* as volume, and volume as *form*. It was associated to wearing a wedding veil, a bishop's miter, a crown. The *head center* evoked regality, *space* opened like halls through Versailles or driving on a highway through Americas western states with miles and miles of open country.

Centers connected associatively with various dance disciplines: *upper chest center* with the Cecchetti ballet carriage; *upper back center* with the Russian ballet carriage; *front middle center* with jazz technique; *Low middle center* with Bournonville, Danish ballet technique, or with folk dancing; *low front and back center* with African folk dance; the Afro-Cuban with *low back center; Graham* with *middle, middle center*. I could see how *Centers* came to exemplify a particular emotional point of departure for each technique. I grasped how "chakras" could come to represent fundamental sources of power, of health, of understandings. I found *Centers* to elicit a powerful *fixed* perspective that held significant value for movement for actors, for developing their plasticity.

Every one of these explorations done over a number of weeks with appropriate supportive music shifted their unconsciously habituated body carriage. It filtered into a better understanding of personal postures, of the physical choices that develop for individuals. The exploration of Centers: *high/head, chest/upper torso, middle navel/lower torso,* and *low/coccyx* and *sacrum/perineum* were reminiscent of clothing periods: Empire, Regency, 1940s waistline skirts, seventies hip huggers, and so on.

Centers had social ethnographic impact. Every exploration heightened their awareness of their own particular physical preference, physical sensibility eliciting unconscious psychological material that began to be shared as a group for the last fifteen minutes of the class. By sharing verbally, a group dynamic evolved. As an aside, I recall a jazz class with a couple of ballet dancers looking totally out of place because of their training. They got the sequence, the timing, but their Centers were too high, so the core of their *form* was off.

After exploring these Centers individually, I began to combine them enhancing the much sought-after *sense of form* that had been so elusive. I believed I had established a creative movement approach to space, eliciting a more sensory experience of the studio space where the arithmetic dimensions never changed, but the *feel of the space* altered because of the changes in Centers. The four Centers: *high, chest, middle, and low,* took a whole year to explore and constituted my creative movement approach to Space, the fourth element of my schema that all dance techniques encompass.

I also began to use Centers for private movement therapy sessions to open up psychosomatically *fixated* emotional life. The client's associations opened their physical fixations and, in turn, how they hardened around a particular area of their body. It served an emotional abreaction, a physical release of the *fixated center*. Although the person found the release experientially meaningful, it was never fully integrated, and thus remained an intellectual level insight. I will speak of this later. Gratified by my continuing creative movement findings for the elements that constitute all dance, I began to focus on the last area – time.

Advanced Level – Time

Time that we all know as seconds, minutes, hours, and so on is traditionally explored in dance with music. The steps and movements of a waltz or following the phrasing of a nocturne, or by accented rhythms in a jazz class or Afro-Cuban dance class. The Time element is the expression of the emotional sense that is being conveyed. In a song it's the verse, in a musical it's the overture. In James Bond films it is The Time of danger, quick trigger reactions, and sexy interludes. Ingmar Bergman has an unusually long shot in the opening of the movie *Anna* of an old massive oak tree, conveying something powerful, aged and unmovable, before taking the viewer into the house of a couple, tired of each other's presence, each other's habits, the material of unmovable personality: Bergman's vision of these couples. The totally steady extended shot sets the tempo of the movie, the grinding interchanges between the couple that will eventually break the surface of sophisticated pretense. That long opening shot served the same purpose as an overture to an opera.

Most dance techniques follow this approach in their training, emphasized by dynamics, like a sudden twist or shift in the body, a rhythmic accent. You may recognize it by interminable turns in place, or space, or skips when children are feeling joyous.

As in the exploration of Space, I wanted to find an exercise, an exploration that elicits an inner sense of time that wasn't dictated externally, like a time shift from being in the mountains, or by the seashore, or governed by the emotional tempo of the household we grow up in.

I had noted that in the exploration of *Space* through *Centers* in the body, the breathing feels different with each *Center*. As I thought about how the breath alters the experience of Centers, I came up with seven breathing patterns to explore time.

These were all explored, as with the Centers, by first laying on their backs on the floor, imaging the lines through the body to then focus on the following seven breaths: 1) High nose breathing rising through the upper part of the nostrils, entering the skull and passing through the back of the neck into the lungs and expanding the back. It's the breathing of a sound sleep, slow, relaxed, a regal bearing; 2) Nose breathing moving through the upper throat evoking a more focused attention to an action, a more pronounced emotional tempo; 3) Nose and throat, as if being rushed through a task or an intention; 4) Throat breathing, as if exercising strongly; 5) Throat and upper chest, getting closer to panting, huffing and puffing; 6) Chest breathing, a held upper chest body, pushing oneself, a contained ferocity, like an unacknowledged anger;

7) Belly breathing, like a complete letting go, a night out at a disco or anywhere where this is accepted. These last two are incredibly physical. We have all experienced these different breaths more or less unconsciously because our awareness is more action focused. We let the breath change on its own, which it does without us having to think about it. The characterizations I've given are very general, because each one of us experiences these various breathing patterns differently, meaning that we have varying attitudes about and expressed in each of these breaths

Breaths are constantly changing, varying with changes in our emotions, most often imperceptibly, and most consciously by activities. Breathing is constantly in flux. The more fixated a particular breathing pattern becomes the more unchanging is the person's sense of *time*. I recall having my arm draped over my wife's rib cage as she slept to sense her breathing change three or four times within seconds giving me the sense of how much our breath is connected to what is going on below the surface.

In recalling, I marvel at the creative intuition arising out of a rather literal way of thinking. I marvel at how they ended up paralleling ancient wisdom that approached these elements from a spiritual and philosophic perspective. What didn't change was my assessment, my anticipation as to how I hoped it would free their improvisational movement language. Was experiencing their altered sense of time coming through on a movement level, was the movement resonating their feelings, or were they still involved with interpreting, giving meaning to the movement language?

Evaluation

These studies took me through the early nineteen eighties. The value of all of these explorations, I came to realize, was impacting on the musculature, because just as the *Centers* moved down the body or the *Breath* moved from nose to stomach, the musculature was affected to one degree or another. Their conscious awareness of the musculature was inconsequential in comparison with the psychological value of each person discovering their predilection for a particular *Center* or *Breath,* discovering habituated bodily and breathing patterns, indicative of their psychological character. Although intellectually stimulating, their movement language remained essentially unchanged.

The Continuing Struggle

I began my movement journey wanting to express myself through dance, a wordless subjective language that I thought reached across cultural boundaries. Was I unconsciously trying to find a road back to a place where muscles and nerves form the dance of feelings? This wordless desire continually drove my creative efforts to discover the primitive language of feelings. If the creative exploration didn't elicit feelings then something was still wrong, something was missing.

When the movement language remained repetitive, *fixation* seemed like a legitimate way to describe the person's emotional cocoon. Their associative processes stimulated their mind, but their movement did not express the excitement of their thoughts or sensations.

Centers and breaths stimulated sentient experiences that felt extraordinary, but the movement language remained moored. What each one of these explorations did was to activate the musculature in those areas, enlisting a more bodily experience, but the motion of movement did not pass through from feet to fingertips, as the head and neck were held, fixed, self-observing. Dance was not happening. It was more the thinking that they found engaging. It was a kind of delusion, an unwitting reinforcement of the magic of thinking, the pride of thought.

Conclusion

As I mentioned early on in this odyssey, the feet, the arch, the 4th toe line, narrowing the stance, shortening the stride, and on to, eventually, the flat, or middle of the heels, the symmetry of sensation, the incremental way of sensing motion tactilely kept taking more and more center stage in my teaching. As in Genesis, the breath that Elohim breathed into Adam gave him life. This practicality diminished the evocative intellectual formulations that had driven my work for so many years.

It is muscles that move the bones. It is the alignment of muscles that facilitates tactile continuity, engendering feelings. It is the interplay between muscles that creates an organic line, form, variation of muscle tonus, evokes space and time. It finally seemed so obvious.

What took me so long to recognize the obvious? "There is nothing new under the sun," Ecclesiastes, tell us. This recognition of the *interplay of muscles,* of the *continuous loop of motion* of which we only need to be aware, rather than guide, initiated the organic movement language that breathed soul and emanated feelings as clearly as the sun lights the universe. Each improvisation is different, as each day is different. It cannot be memorized. Each one of us must rekindle the sequence of the *tactile interplay, the loop of the tactile interplay,* anew each time. The practical becomes the truth.

None of us is privileged by the past.

Dance is an expression of feelings constantly changing, as they do in life. Life, we can only speak of in hindsight because it is light passing. You notate it, but that is not its living reality. This awareness humbles us. It is the dance of the unconscious alive in motion. This realization is the reason for the title of the book – **Out of Aloneness.**

CHAPTER 6

PRACTICAL ADVICE FOR EVERYONE

The Only Sensitive Way to Exercise

According to a tongue-in-cheek article by Paul Ingraham, science writer, former massage therapist, and assistant editor of Science-Based Medicine from Vancouver, Canada, there are 50,100,000,701 muscles in the body. He asserts that this is about 99% accurate. This shocking number is attained by his inclusion of millions of tiny hair-raising muscles, and the smooth muscle cells blended together of the stomach and organs that we have no control over. On a voluntary level, we use about 200 muscles that, by how we engage these 200, affect another almost 500 smaller muscles. He caps his summary by stating, "there is exactly one heart muscle."

As I have already shared with you, from early on I had paid no attention to muscles, aside from comparing the size of mine with other adolescent boys, my calves, upper arm, biceps. What captured my attention was whether, when we were in the fourth grade, I could run faster than Boris Rabinovitch, at Centro Israelita, in Habana, Cuba. Then there was my competition with Jimmy Bonno, when we were trying out for the baseball team at Cass Technical High School in Detroit.

Or, as a teenager, an important question for me was whether I could handle tackling my fourteen-year-old friend Don Worsley in our pick-up football scrimmages on Ewald Circle by the catholic high school. Don was already muscular and fast. In comparison with him I felt small and too thin. These are the kinds of judgements of self that adolescents and teenagers worry about. I was coordinated, I could pick up any sport, or learn dance steps without much ado. An inherent sense of rhythm helped me to feel not only adequate but equal, and sometimes even superior. I've come to realize that underlying these developmental comparisons and misgivings is the fear of inadequacy, an active sense of jealousy, and a competitive, if measured, use of aggression.

These adolescent and teen year preoccupations often continue unimpeded into adulthood, perhaps disguised in a "that is the way the world works" attitude, in an effort to mask a righteous self-centeredness. The infant's sense of inadequacy and fear doesn't just vanish. These are not idle inner meanderings, they manifest in characterological movement and behavioral choices, in personal aims as to what kind of exercising is chosen, in overdetermined ideas, too often leading to medically significant problems.

It was only after many years of frustration, working through my judgments, and immense patience in trying to figure out why students were not imitating exercises when they were believing that they were; and many years of looking at improvisations for meaning rather than being moved by feelings, that I finally realized that most students functioned with the notion that they just have to keep doing what they were doing, because *in time* their flexibility and strength would eventually be what they imagined they would be. Their fixation on aim, and the time when their hope or wish would be realized, was greater than the actuality of muscular sensation. In the creative movement section of the class there were similar issues, the disparity between what was being asked for and demonstrated, which they believed they were doing, and what they were actually doing. I was stuck in my observation of how far off their movement was from what I had shown and explained and from what I had hoped the focus of the improvisation would elicit. It was exasperating. This disparity between *belief* and *actuality* brought me to an awareness that lead to the insight of *incremental adjustments*.

Making over 200 muscles work smoothly depends on *sensing the motion of movement through muscles*. It depends on sensing the continuity of motion passing into the adjoining muscles. Since muscle endings (tendons) attach to bones at the junction of joints, sensing the continuity of motion **necessitates incremental torques of the musculature around joints.** These torques, or slight twists, are unique to each person and subtle, but they are practical and necessary to experience the perception of the flow of motion from muscle to muscle. I came to call this process **The Interplay of Muscles.**

Try this slowly, continually sensing the continuity of motion from the tip of the toes through the pelvis and torso, and from the fingertips through the neck.

Please note that the continuity of motion always goes around joints rather than into joints. This always involves a torque, a slight twist in the motion through the musculature. Muscle endings are bound by joints. My technique differs from other techniques in that it requires you to find that slight torque that allows you to perceive the continuity of motion around the joint. This continuity is unconscious. It happens when action, motivation, and feelings flow seamlessly together.

There is no question that in learning to *sense motion* this specifically demands a clear distinction between our tactile and visual self-perception in how we exercise.

Once the *touch* sensitivity of motion within the muscles is awakened (I will detail this in subsequent sections), I can assure you, you'll begin to repair known and unknown misalignments. Self-repair is inevitable if you learn to sense the *interplay of muscles*: the sensation of motion through the muscle as it connects to the adjoining muscles. The process slowly, but permanently, *changes habitual joint aches and pains* that often impact on the musculature affected by stress on the joints. As you *incrementally* realign, pain dissolves, at times without your actually realizing it.

Developing this sensitivity protects you in how you integrate what you're learning from someone else. It is *self-protective* against well-meaning instructors and the demands of coaches formulated out of their experience and their ideals – perspectives to which you may aspire. Aspirations are wishes, mental constructs, self-imaging, that can, and often do, bypass the actuality of tactile, sensory perception of **touch**.

Ideals are concerned with an end result. *Incremental adjustment* is a *subjective process* in how we arrive at those ideals, whether they are positions, figures, steps, dynamics, or whatever makes up those end results. You are the only one who has to integrate, through your perception of motion through muscles, what someone is telling or showing you.

There is no better self-protective approach to exercising than learning how to sense incremental adjustments.

The most far-reaching benefit is that it puts you in touch with a direct transmission of the unconscious energy being given through the silent language of movement. I'll say more about this last point that sounds hard to believe if you've never experienced this or thought in these terms. The simplest example I can think of is babies learn and experience the unconscious of the mother through the silent language of the motion of movement. My sixty years of dealing with this problem has convinced me and all of the students in my classes that it is true. The techniques I've developed emphasize reawakening this sensitivity in adults.

> Cynthia, a psychoanalyst, danced and choreographed during her college years. Now in her fifties, she continued to experience her body with the same love for moving she had when she was much younger. She clearly understood the idea of *incremental* and thought she was doing it. Her need to feel free, to sense looseness, superseded the specificity of an incremental tactile sensation. She "visualized" incremental, as she visualized words, with a quickness of mind and humor that was unmistakable. She demanded quickness, much too much, of herself, which got in the way of the tactile incremental sensitivity. The memory of movement as gratification, as a natural release of tension, superseded, time and again, incremental adjustments. She finally was able to make the distinction between imagining tactile and experiencing tactile by distinguishing the difference in texture. It happened by persistently returning to the contact with the floor.

Let me cite a more general dance example. Second position *port-de-bras* (French for carriage of the arms) in ballet is arms stretched out to the sides of the torso, about chest high – a gesture of welcome or openness. The perfect positioning is how each individual senses the motion from the fingertips through the upper arms and into the shoulders and torso. Because of the differences of individuals, our bones, muscles, and perception, it may require that the arms be somewhat lower than the shoulders or more in front of the chest. Unless this individual *tactile* sensibility of the *Interplay of Muscles* is developed, the *port-de-bras* will always look either too stiff, a demanding openness lacking in warmth, or too limp, pleading in its request for warmth. We understand the intent of the positioned gesture, but the emotional evocation is reduced to a symbol. We guess at what is meant, but we don't feel it. Intent and feeling are simply not the same. Intent invariably stands alone, while feeling evokes an empathic continuity, not only on the interpersonal emotional level, but in the tangible flow of movement.

Another down-to-earth example is a rough carpenter who hammers with his hand, wrist, and forearm, sensing the motion through his upper arm, shoulders, and into his back. If the carpenter isn't sensing the motions, his arm and shoulders become really stiff by the end of the day. Every musician knows full well the problems of a technique that doesn't flow through the whole body. Medical issues are sure to follow unless the *incremental process* happens.

Judges at the Olympics differ in the way they perceive the flow of the motion of the contestants. Some see the flow of gestures, like words in a diary, some see the connection between figures expressing changes in moods, and some resonate to the rhythmic dynamics of excitement, as if in a drama. Underlying these various preferences is each judge's internal emotional sense of what constitutes connectedness.

Anna's foot had been hurting for months, at times bringing her to tears. She visited all sorts of medical specialists, and numerous other health providers in the hope that one of them would make the pain go away. Each treatment helped for a little while, and yet the pain returned. At one point, an MRI seemed to identify the anatomic source of the problem, but the treatment option was short-lived. I was aware of the fact that she had grown up with a mom who had a life-long physically inhibiting condition. Her medical effort was to find the reason for her pain and each professional asserted their notion of the reason. Why didn't any of the help last?

I was conscious of the mother-daughter link. Unfortunately, the mind-body link regarding her pain escaped her. The flexibility that a lifetime of yoga had given her, to ensure that she would not end up like her mother, overshadowed the practicality of the suggestions I had made over the years. This time, the urgency of her pain allowed her to relate to the **specifics** of what I asked her to try.

We spent at least a half hour doggedly making incredibly small incremental adjustments affecting the feet, her stance, and a slight pelvic twist that relaxed her lower back until she perceived without question the sensation of motion through the muscles.

"The pain has disappeared." She smiled. "Great, you have to sustain what you're sensing into your walk." As soon as the words came out of my mouth, she immediately began to backtrack. "I'm going to look peculiar. I don't want people to ask me, 'What is wrong with your body?'"

Her comment reinforced, for my analytic ear, the pain's unconscious connection to the physically impaired mother from whom she could still not separate. Her tendency to experience herself in relationship with others was a trademark of her therapeutic skill, but it thwarted a direct connection to practical tactile motion and thus to her own feelings. Her particular sensitivity to relationships was greater than to her own bodily sensation and her own feelings.

Each of us has to find a way to sense our feelings to genuinely separate from the caring object, usually the mother. This separation allows us to maintain a feeling relationship to our mother that recognizes her feelings. There is no substitute for this very subjective process. It is often a lifetime process, worth the courage of the effort.

Her backtracking is a good example of psychological fixations. It takes more than the blaring sounds of horns that broke down the Walls of Jericho to break the walls of fixations!

To help her not revert to her former unconscious habits, I had her slide the foot into a step very slowly so she would not lose what she had successfully managed to sense. She couldn't sustain her own self-healing experience. The unconscious connection to the mother, for whom she was the ear that listened, was still too enveloping.

Anna surprised me when, a week later, she had an insight into her mother's disavowal of her physical impairment. She could see it about her mother but couldn't yet see it about herself. The fact of seeing the denial was already an improvement.

This is a perfect example of a mother's unconsciously maintained attitude that is unconsciously taken in by her daughter. She transformed this rigid attitude through a reaction formation, doing the opposite, by exercises for flexibility. She did this with recognition of why it was important to her and where it came from. Yet she was unable to sustain her intellectual awareness by remaining connected to a process that relieved her of pain. The family never spoke about the mother's impairment, which was as obvious as the nose on your face – a familial collusion of disavowal about physicality and its emotional implications for the self and others. Toddlers, profoundly invested in their physical acquisitions and the freedom that follows, pick up on this emotional denial.

All of us sense this inter-psychic connection with another person. We all have this sensitivity built into our brain's *mirror neurons*. Our muscles are actually responsive to the motion of someone we're observing. This inborn sensitivity is an invaluable to our survival as infants, helping us adapt and adjust to the vibrations around and inside us. You have to understand that this is going on all the time, most often below the surface of attention.

Although this sensitivity is always operating, for most people it remains unrecognized and, unfortunately, disconnected from their physicality. There are always special moments when this sensitivity rises to the surface – love, an unusually striking sunrise or sunset, or surround, or the anguish of a deep loss. We all recognize these moments as something more than our usual experience of emotions. We lose our boundaries; the frames of space and time vanish in those moments.

Every skill invariably brings this sensitivity into play by focusing on the smooth workings of their practice along the lines of how things should work. It becomes a principle of efficiency and a driving force in the elimination of resistance. I believe that it is an extension of this in-born part of us.

When it comes to exercising, sensing *incrementally* the *interplay* is the **only totally personal way to work**, regardless of what kind of exercise is being done. I will deal with the *Interplay* more extensively in a subsequent section. It protects us from strains, sprains, and tears. It alleviates physical disconnections that develop because of our right or left-handed preference, or because of accidents, or imitation of the person we wanted to be like. Children learn by imitating. Adults, however, have the capacity to be conscious, and the patience to be sensitive.

It is this emotional sensitivity that helps us to sense continuity in the flow of any action, be it tennis, folding egg whites, or listening. Teaching and correcting *incrementally* was a difficult transition for me, steeped as I was in the energy charged physical release of tension and anticipation of excitement that dominates the field of dance. Those underlying determinants drove me over the many years I spent dancing seven to ten hours of every day. It is only in retrospect that I can acknowledge how maniacally I defended this exhausting way of living, defending against my fear of depressive feelings, of living a sad life. Excitement, which I was capable of channeling artistically, was more engrossing than what I felt.

Witnessing this *incremental* flow is unmistakable. The corroboration from the community of students, all highly individualistic, has convinced me that although the *incremental flow* is spoken about in similes, metaphors, and concepts that sound different from each other, there is always agreement about the movement itself. We all sense the organic *incremental* process. Almost sixty years into teaching creative movement, along with my practice as a psychoanalyst, has convinced me that it is a part of our collective emotional hardwiring.

There simply is no substitute for learning to sense *tactilely*, and thus *incrementally*, to heal both physically and emotionally. It is the practical transformative approach for body and feelings to come together.

SYMMETRY

The idea of symmetry began with becoming aware of what the body does when exercising. If the arms are lifted to stretch to the left, the right arm and side are pulling to the left. The left side musculature therefore contracts to keep balance. The arms are reaching out to the left side while the body is grabbing on the left side. This is an inherent contradiction between the wish expressed by the gesture and the fear of the loss of balance in reaching out so far that we lose the solidity of the grounded feet to the floor.

> *Try this slowly to sense the distinction between palms facing each other or both palms facing the direction of the stretch.*

Unwittingly, the mind is given opposing considerations, right side extends, while left side controls for balance. Obviously, some people focus on the stretch, while others focus on the control of staying balanced. This contrasting problem is true of every exercise because the musculature works that way. For every muscle that stretches, there is an opposing muscle that contracts, referred to as agonist and antagonist.

The problem is psychological. The wish is connected to the gesture that is reaching. The reaching gesture is the expression of the feeling. To promote the feeling throughout the body, I suggested that as the right arm with palm down extending, requires the left palm should twist left rather than remain facing the right palm. As a result, the whole body becomes engaged in the wish/feeling of the gesture without a contradictory sensation.

Remember – incremental adjustment.

This approach promotes moving into space as the whole musculature is engaged in the expression of the wish/gesture. Movement, the feeling and the continuity of feelings, becomes more important than the meaning of the gesture. This practical suggestion promoted a conscious awareness of the exercise, reinforcing *Creative Movement,* with its focus on improvisation. It kept the body and the mind more together. When I applied this way of exercising to the very beginning of sensing the *flat of the heels*, the perception of the *symmetry of sensation* between right and left middle of the heels became essential in the realignment process between right and left feet, ankles, calves, and so on.

You can well imagine how symmetry promoted realignment, constantly correcting the unconscious habits that develop for each one of us, that over time result in aches, pain, and, finally, medical interventions.

Symmetry like *incremental* become fundamental in promoting the *Interplay of Muscles* that leads to the transcending moment when quantity moves into quality, when movement as actions becomes the expression of our unconscious – a flow of feelings with no interruptions, always new and surprising, the essence of creativity.

THE FLAT OF THE HEELS

The most recent discovery

An intuitive suggestion turned into a discovery. It took place just a few years ago.

Ted developed a lung condition that landed him in the hospital. When he returned to class, although he paced himself well during the exercises, my biggest concern was his tendency to cut off his breath by reacting to the music with an unconscious immediacy, and willful self-righteous justification, "It's what the music is conveying." I, on the other hand, looked at him as "jumping into the music, with a disregard for the incremental interplay of muscles."

I would see the immediate tightening of muscles around his chest and mouth as he lunged into the music, taxing his breathing. My efforts over the years to have him stay with his musculature more consciously in his spontaneous engagement with the music had been only partially successful. The immediacy of his tendency was so strong that I worried for his lungs, especially after his hospital stay.

Intuitively, I looked down to his feet and suggested, "Try to continually to step over the flat of the heels as you move," a reference I had used somewhat differently in the past, when in an effort to have the students continue their awareness of stepping over the *fourth toe line* on the sole of their feet, I asked them to slide the feet out on the floor as they stepped forward into a walk to help sustain the sensitivity of staying over the *4th toe line of the feet*.

I explained my concern about his breathing, wanting him to not tax himself in this first class after his hospitalization. He often sparred with me in class, as if what I was suggesting was my projection, my demand that he move the way I thought was right. Implicit in his dismissals of my focal suggestions, by treating it as my psychological projection, was a negation of the musculature through which our sensing *must* happen. It was always annoying, though I understood his competitive anger. His mind was a source of great strength in overcoming significant physical pain over a lifetime.

But then, all at once, thank goodness, it worked. He listened to what I was suggesting, accepting my concern wholeheartedly and without any quips. I was surprised and amazed as I looked at him doing exactly what I had suggested, and the difference it made in the way the music flowed through him, as it never had before. His physical childhood impairment, which drove the compensatory quickness of his physicality, disappeared, vanished into thin air. This new way of moving was in stark contrast to his "jumping into the music." My psychoanalytic interpretation of his intrepid nature was that making his body react so quickly to the music is a somaticized way of dealing with the fear of his body collapsing during childhood. His intrepid determination to overcome the childhood physical impairment played a significant role in his accomplishments, but in this particular situation I feared it was aggravating his lung condition.

Because I was stunned by how the motion was moving through his body by virtue of his paying attention to the *flat of the heels*, I quickly asked that everyone also move with the constancy of the ***flat of the heels***. For some reason, everyone totally understood what I meant by the flat of the heels. The results were remarkable. They all moved with the same total physical awareness that I had noticed in Ted. The *flat of the heel* focus resonated through their musculature emanating an organic flow of feelings through every motion in every movement. I could see the improvised movement rising from the un-thought depths of every person. I couldn't get over it. It was a eureka moment.

I was delighted to note that the focus on the *flat of the heels* results in stepping over *the 4th toe line of the feet automatically*, as well as placing the pelvis over the heels naturally as they moved. It affected the organic flow of weight transference in each person's improvisation, eliciting feelings that appeared without intent. It confirmed my sense that the *musculature is the highway of the unconscious*.

The flat of the heels is a magical elixir.

INSTRUCTION
        (Remember – incrementally)

Here is what to look for as you try to experience the middle of the heels:

- Sit on a straight back chair so that you can place your feet flat on the floor. Sit forward on the chair to help to place your heels flat on the floor.
- Note what part of your heels you sense. Is it the inside or outside of the heel? Or is the middle part of the heel totally clear on one foot but not on the other? You're awakening your perception about the heel contact with the floor. You probably have never paid attention to exactly what part of your heels you sense on the floor. Note the difference in your perception between right and left heels.
- **Do not make changes too quickly.** Paying such close attention to this perceptual process can easily tax your patience. Impatience has a lot to do with wishing. It is the insistence of wanting to know **right away** what something is about, so you can take care of it – right away.
- Is the sensation of the left heel more on the inside? If so, then **incrementally** move your left leg in closer to right leg until you have a better sense of the middle of the heel. If the sensation of the right leg is more on the inside, then **incrementally** bring the leg in closer to the center, until you sense the flat of the heel more clearly. The asymmetry between right and left leg is pretty common. Just make the adjustments slowly, until you can sense the middle of the heels on both feet, and the sensation feels symmetrical.
- You may still sense the outside of either the right or the left leg. DO NOT MOVE THE HEELS. Slowly swivel the right or left knee in towards the center of the body. You will immediately sense the flat of the heel.

- Finding the flat of the heels may surprise you. Try swiveling back and forth until you can easily return to the flat of heels, establishing a retrievable memory of the sensation of the flat of the heels. A retrievable memory affects our sense of security. Don't worry too much about it. You will have to retrieve the flat of the heels *anew* each time you stand, which I assure you will eventually take only a second.
- This particular adjustment will possibly give you the sense of tightening the space around your groin. Take a moment to pitch your torso forward, giving you a sense of lifting your torso up. This adjustment will lift your lumbar vertebrates, the lower 5 bones in the spine that tend to round as you sit. This will automatically pitch your torso up and forward. The muscles from the groin to below the navel will begin to contract and support your lower back that may have given you problems.

You're on the way to healing

- Take a long moment to register the changes in sensation in your musculature. You have and are changing the way your legs fit into the pelvic sockets. **Please, don't rush.**
- The essence of my approach is that adjustments and changes must happen without any tightening. If you feel stiffening, you are not working incrementally. The aim of every adjustment is easy to imagine. The whole point of this work is becoming alive to the sensation, not the aim or purpose of the work, but the sensing in the event.

- When stiffening happens, generally the sensation of motion has changed from *tactile* to *visual.*
- This tendency is common. Simply go back to the sensation of motion before the tightening happened, making sure to sense the contact with the ground – our true source of support.
- Visualization is imaging a sensation. It is an *as if* sensation. This is what I did for years, because I was in a hurry trying to impress with how quickly I got what was being asked for. It didn't take long for me to sprain my left ankle. As the years passed without proper instruction, just constantly lifting up against the strain, it eventually affected my knee, left buttock, and lower back. **Be careful in how you sense these changes.** If you remain sensitive to the *tactile* sensation, sustaining it as it moves around the ankle and into the outside of your calves, you will correct problems around the knees, hip, and lower back forever. I will deal with standing, in the next section.

The flat of the heels is the most important center of balance.

- You have to get used to finding it each time anew. I can only assure you that you will be profoundly rewarded physically and emotionally. It may sound philosophic, but what you are getting used to is sensing what is actually happening on a muscular level physically in the NOW. The flow of feelings and of thought continues within the context of the muscular motion awareness.

This process is a profound change in our usual perceptual sensory development. It is highly personal. It is very specific. It must not be rushed. Take your time establishing this perceptual sensitivity. Little by little it happens more quickly and closer to our accustomed sense of timing, the tendency for our intent and wish to quickly come together, as we imagined it did when we were infants. The amount of time for this awareness to be integrated emotionally will vary with each individual. It may take months, or even years, to effect this change emotionally. However, I can assure you, it will happen. Don't give up. Whatever degree of change you make, following this incremental process is always for the better. The tactile process of motion begins to compliment the usual process of intent that we are so accustomed to. Beside repairing the physical issues that plague so many of us as we age, we are rewarded by the accompanying natural evocation of feelings, not as emotions that tend to stop us, but by the flow of feelings.

The Phoenix rises from the ashes of the unconscious in which it had unwittingly settled. You will celebrate its rebirth.

STANDING

Into the World of Equals

Standing is a monumental achievement. When the infant grabs a hold of the protective slats around the crib and pulls itself up to standing, it must be comparable to Edmund Hillary reaching the pinnacle of Mount Everest. These discoveries for infants are emotionally monumental. When the infant looks at its arm rising for the first time and repeats this act numerous times before it ever registers as volition, how could it be anything but colossal in the wordless level of experience.

These achievements are more than the discovery of control, they are acts of flight, magical ascensions into the ether. These are mythological experiences and achievements that only gods would be capable of. When the unbroken body-spirit arm rises, floating away, who knows where it will then descend to touch the blanket. It is a magical moment in feeling alive, celebrated as the first prayer by Orthodox Jews, thanking god for returning their soul to them. It is the awakening of sensation out of the quantum world of constantly changing arrangement of particles, vortices of energy, the world of flux, of impermanence.

On a more literal level I am reminded of an acquaintance, many years ago, a tenor guitarist from Columbia, South America, a descendant of the illustrious Sassoon family, the Rothschild family of the Middle East. We discovered soon after meeting him that he did gigs for headliners as an opening act in Las Vegas. He was a very accomplished guitarist with a wealth of musical material. A few months into our friendship we discovered that his proudest accomplishment was not his musicianship, but doing miniature-size, 8 x 8inch versions of the luminous oil paintings of Johannes Vermeer. The first time he showed us a few of these metallic miniature pieces, we were taken aback by how exquisitely perfect the reproductions were. It is not easy to reduce big to small, or vice versa, in painting. The graphic detailing of colors requires a delicate eye, let alone teaching himself to mix the egg whites into the oils that made Vermeer's oils so luminous. These miniatures were his crowning accomplishment. It was, in hindsight, his infant arm descending unto the sheet of his crib, a return of his soul not bound by entertaining or applause. It was his monumental achievement. Standing for an infant is a fantastic, glorious act of motion, as all the muscles move for them to rise up on their feet. It has to register on an unconscious sensory level as standing on the peak of Mount Everest, as the perfect Vermeer reproduction, as an act of ascension.

(Incrementally. Only as much as you can do without tensing.)

INSTRUCTIONS

- Start by sitting on a straight back chair, so that your buttock is not collapsing into the seat. Please stand and sit down a few times until you've gotten some sense of what is happening in your body as you stand and sit.
- If, while paying attention, you stand up the way most of us have been doing since infancy, you will immediately notice that you probably have leaned forward, have pushed inward into the pelvic joints, thrust your spine upwards with your head leading the way, and with your eyes focused by your intent to stand you probably sense a slight satisfaction in accomplishing what you set out to do. You will notice as you return to sitting how you stick your buttock back, as if it has eyes looking for the chair.
- You have done this so often over a lifetime of standing and sitting that it seems totally right. Through these repetitions of standing and sitting you're taking stock of and acknowledging your habits.

(Notice how you naturally stand and sit)

Our *intent*, our wish to stand is so unconsciously focused that the *flat of the heels, the contact with floor* is simply not considered. This is a perfect example of *splitting.* Although the sensation of motion through the muscles is still happening, our aim is split off from the tactile awareness. Our intent totally overshadows the sensations of motion. Our mind makes use of body memory, bypassing a sensitivity to our own sensory process. The *wish* is stronger than the feeling-sensation. We unconsciously *use* the body, but no longer sense it. ***This is the crux of our dissociative development.*** We are not even aware of because we've been doing it for so long. It happens unconsciously, we have forgotten what sensing is about. We become focused on aims and motivations – this is the hollowness of mind over matter.

- Now that I have pointed out the problem, you need to revisit standing. You may remember my story about Bailah after her stroke. I kept putting my palm gently over her neck to help her to sense the sole of her feet pushing into the floor, forcing her to experience the sensation of contact rising into her calves and thighs. It was this strengthening exercise that helped her to a relatively quick recovery. I hadn't at that point arrived at the *flat of the heel* discovery. Nevertheless, the technique worked beautifully to strengthen her leg muscles. You need to do the same thing.
- Sit again, reestablish the *flat of the heels,* taking as long as necessary to do so. BE PATIENT. There is nothing wrong with the *wish*, it simply should not supersede *the tactile process.*
- Sit forward on the chair. Now continually lean forward with your head and torso towards the floor, lower than

you have ever thought was necessary to stand, until the contact of the *flat of the heels* with the floor feels unquestionable. If you are heavy, and your stomach is large, just go as far forward as you can. This may affect your sense of balance, so do it slowly. Rise slowly pushing into the flat of the heels so that you sense the sensation of contact moving from the floor through your feet into the calves and into the back of your thighs. As you try standing in this way a few times, you will feel yourself rising, getting taller as the torso lifts fully. You will be experiencing the sensation of motion as an ascension, as if it was happening to you, although you know rationally that you are doing it! What you'll have to admit to is that they are both true! You are doing it and it is happening to you! The you that perceives with and without a body. You can call it the ghost or the abstracted god within. It is a part of self that we should never dismiss.

(Try this incrementally)

- Small children experience themselves in this self-reflexive way. Admittedly it falls away as they become increasingly focused on the intent of an action, which is reinforced by being rushed, until the intent, the purpose, overshadows their sensation, their sensory self-experience. Nevertheless, the self-reflexive experience still rears its head when we are moved by a feeling, touched by someone or something. It is essentially the **feeling** of the movement along **with** its intent. If you can stop and think about it, *sensing the motion* and *our intent* are *mutually inclusive*. When you get used to how inclusive this process is, everything you do is fuller, richer as it is happening. The *splitting* of *wish from feeling* ends.

I hope you'll forgive the repetition. Some might find it patronizing and trying. Experience has taught me the need to repeat these instructions, because our attention's agility is so entrenched in our behavior, what I call the *wishing mind*. The significance of the wishing mind is its quickness, an essential component for dealing with danger. The fear of danger is forgotten but the quickness of reactions remains, and we treat this quickness as a positive aspect of intelligence. This is an example of how unconsciously our mind reverses a negative into a positive. It makes suspicion seem smart, rather than what in this case it is, namely: the quickness of blocking an openness to what is being felt.

- Once you've repeatedly experienced standing over the *flat of the heels*, you are ready to make further incremental adjustments.
- Please, notice if the arch of either foot has slightly collapsed.
- You'll sense more tension on the inside of the ankle of the collapsed arch.
- Usually only one of the arches collapses slightly more, while the other feels totally firm. I suggest toeing-in the foot in which the arch collapses, by swiveling the toes in without moving the heel, until standing on the flat of the heels is **symmetrical** on both heels.

It may surprise you to realize how unevenly you have gotten used to standing, how much you favor one leg and put more pressure on that leg and less on the other. This the essence of misalignments, buttock and lower back issues.

(Try this incrementally. Do not force the changes)

- This unevenness is the source of all the aches and pains that travel up the body to compensate. Discovering the asymmetry and changing it is based on the irrefutable *sensation of contact* with the floor, a sensation *based on touch,* our earliest developing sense as a fetus. This sensation allows you to *incrementally* realign the musculature from the feet upwards.
- I should mention at this point, that as you follow the sensation of motion through the muscles, the blockages in the continuity of *tactile motion* always occur around a joint. Joints tend to stiffen for balance, which is the reason that you may pull at joints for flexibility. The way of exercising for flexibility that I have discovered is sensing the continuity of *tactile motion* around a joint, closer to the actual construction of the body. Once again, the tendency to do something quickly, stiffening to straighten for example, tightens joints. And this eventually leads to medical interventions when sensation becomes painful and intolerable.
- It brings to mind, Gwen Vernon, the incomparable Broadway star of "Redhead," telling me how she asked to have a nerve cut that was causing her so much pain. Dancers ask so much of their body, work so hard for so many years to have it available for whatever they *wish* to do that they go through really difficult operations and hopeful recoveries because they weren't trained with the

tactile sensibility that is truly subjective, but unfortunately takes time. The problem is not just training. It is, as I mentioned earlier, an endemic problem that we all have, **quickness** of thought, the hallmark of arrogance. It is the source of stress – period.

A word about balance. We have a built-in balance system. The inner ear and brain combine to tell muscles what to do to balance the body. It is not exactly the same, but we are like cats in the balance sense. Now, balance doesn't care whether we are aligned or not. It is a survival mechanism not involved in feelings. It does what it can, as best it can. The more efficient the continuity of tactile motion, the greater the suspension of balance. Break dancers discover continuity by moving into and out of joints so quickly they approximate the absolute freedom of unhampered flow. They impress us by their articulation, eliciting admiration, but do not touch us emotionally. We reward them with dollars, like the flame blower on the street.

Let's return to standing.

- You are realigning the musculature on that leg slowly and changing the source of ankle, knee, hip and lower back problems – forever.
- If the *interplay of muscles* does not align through the middle of the pelvis, the torso compensates. You will either lean forward towards the front of the *flat of the heels* or towards the back of the *flat*. The beginning ache in the lower back is the eventual telltale symptom.
- The adjustments to stand over the center of the heel, commonly doesn't take long. The biggest problem is psychological – impatience.

- Keep making the very personal *incremental* adjustments that makes the symmetry of the sensation of standing over the flat of the heels unmistakable.

The 4ᵀᴴ TOE LINE

The Base for Motion

The *4th toe line on the sole of the feet* was the first significant alignment discovery I made. I was absolutely thrilled when I realized how helpful it was in initiating a better sense of motion through muscles.

Prior to my specific focus on *4th toe line* discovery in the early 1980s, the focus of the exercises was a more general attention to flexibility and strength. I considered these as fundamental to executing all the more formal demands of steps and figures of the various dance techniques, including ballet, modern dance, jazz, Afro-Cuban. Flexibility promoted a more fluid sense of *line* and strength promoted a sharper sense of *form*. The exercises proceeded as I have already detailed in an earlier section, from gross stretching of torso, upper body, arms, shoulders, neck, starting from a sitting position on the floor. This was what distinguished the modern dance approach from the verticality of ballet training, allowing for easier stretching by not having to worry about balance. The sitting accentuated pulling the torso upward away from the buttocks, opening the fluidity and strength of the spine, liberating it from the legs to increase the stretch of the legs away from the pelvic joint. This is a particularly important distinction for modern dance to encourage a familiarity and use of all of space, especially the floor, to show emotions from defeat, to anxiety, to obstinacy, to express more graphically and spatially feelings than in ballet, where the expression was limited to more of a miming. Over the years these spatial innovations have crossed into all sorts of dance forms.

Looking back, I can say, without equivocation, that emphasizing the floor was a general way to limber up the body. However, the emphasis, whether stated or not, encourages distending the musculature away from the bones to which they are attached, unwittingly reinforcing misalignments and eventual weakening the body structurally. Persistently trying to stretch away from the bones weakens the solidity of the body which the muscles brace for stability. When problems arise, most people have no sense that the way they used their body led to the problem. It is unfortunately too often treated as bad luck, accompanied by a "learn to live with it" attitude.

The placement of the sole of the feet running from the heel towards the 4th toe strengthens the arch of the feet, the springboard for lightness, for softness, for the sense of motion moving from the floor through the legs and pelvis into the torso and neck. It strengthens kinesiology's principle that oppositional muscles work in tandem – meaning, that for every muscle that elongates there is a muscle that shortens. Exercising, in this way keeps flexibility and strength developing together for greater security and self-protection. It keeps body and soul as partners in movement expression. It goes a long way in repairing physical issues that seemed intractable. By keeping the body safe and grounded, the erratic part of our spirit, violence can be safely expressed without injury to the self or to others, instead of being contained by pulling into the musculature and joints, with inevitable impairment.

My insight into standing over the *4th toe line on the sole of the feet* came about while I was helping Miriam, a social worker, over fifty, with flat fallen arches. No bone deformation, just bad habits, progressively worsening over a lifetime. The non-existent arches persistently betrayed the longing for freedom of her spirit.

> We sat across from each other for a private session, as I showed her how to slowly make the changes that would allow her to sense the 4th toe alignment. It took repeated incremental adjustments over the course of an hour for her to even begin to differentiate the sensation of an arch through the forty muscles and twenty-seven bones of each foot that must adjust to each other. She never got to the full correction, but enough to encourage her to continue to improve in the class and hopefully in her life.
>
> This grounding effort helped to offset lifting her rib cage, shoulders and head, pulling at her neck, to express her excitement dancing. Miriam's lengthy psychotherapy liberated her wish for physical freedom, her wish to fly, but her body couldn't support it. Imagine wings that cannot catch the air for lift. The freedom was literally truncated above the pelvis.

The *fourth toe line placement* became a mantra to help students sense motion in the muscles of the feet in all of the standing exercises. The *4th toe alignment* became a significant starting point to alter the way that students, tending to copy me during the exercise portion of the class, were affecting a more conscious *"tactile"* sense of their muscles. Prior to the *4th toe* focus, my corrections on different parts of the body went on for years, as my frustration increased, because I couldn't understand why the corrections were not being permanently integrated. The disparity between *belief* and *actuality* was frustrating and the 4th toe placement began to narrow that gulf.

For years, I thought of flexibility and strength as the reasons for exercising, assuming that their movement vocabulary as they improvised would be more creative, more interesting. I didn't really consider that their insecurity in taking more physical chances was based on their *misalignments.* Over time, the body, via the vestibular system, the balance system kept making compensatory muscular corrections leading to habituated misalignments. Bringing the 4th toe placement to consciousness initiated a practical tactile process that put the person in charge of sensing when the motion of movement wasn't continuing smoothly. They began to learn the specific place in their body that required a special attention, a specific torque for realignment.

We *imagine* our body, visualizing movement without ever sensing the motion within the muscles. We somehow believe that we are naturally connected, that everything works together. How else would our physical gifts have developed? The physical compensations that our balance system accommodates through compensations seems to be enough. But it isn't.

Mary, a wonderful, gifted artist, big, and heavy-bodied, moved physically through space with no sense of her musculature. She was emotionally committed to the enjoyment of moving, the wishing spirit of her soul.

She wasn't alone. This applied to most of my adult students.

I tried to understand by coming up with the usual excuses for their limitations: too old, pre-existing problems, inaptitude, lack of talent, or unconscious resistance to my authority. All of the aforementioned explanations have a modicum of truth about them, but they are useless from a physical reparative perspective. The excuses are dismissive, arrogant, or sympathetic, social, psychological, cultural, but they don't change a thing.

How could I teach them to sense muscles? Is there a physical perception that doesn't have to be imagined?

This is where the *contact to the floor* came into play. The contact of our feet to the floor is immediate. It doesn't have to be imagined. It is like our fingers touching a surface, unquestionable. It is in the **NOW**.

I began to ask questions:

Can you sense your feet touching the ground?

If you stand over the fourth toe line on the sole of the feet can you feel the arch of the feet automatically rising without bracing the sole of the feet inward into the ankles to lift the arch?

Can you perceive the sensation of touch, of contact with the ground moving through the muscles of your feet?

If you **swivel** one or both your toes in slightly, does it improve the clarity of the 4th toe placement? can you sense the muscles with no stiffening of the toes or ankles as you lift the heels?

Can you continually step over the 4th toe line as you walk? If you **narrow** the distance between your legs, does it make it easier to not lose the sense of the 4th toe line?

If you **shorten** your stride as you step into a walk, does it help to continuously step over the 4th toe line of your feet? If you can continue to step over the 4th toe line, can you sense the motion of movement rising into the calves and thighs more easily?

Try to dance to the music without losing your perception of the 4th toe line contact with the floor no matter what your body does.

These observations posed as questions and incremental adjustments engraved the **4th toe line** in my consciousness.

The clarity of motion through the feet's muscular connections were either sensed or not. Changes could be made *incrementally*. Small personal adjustments constantly tested by *the internal sensation of motion through muscles* became more and more alive.

I called the clarity of motion connecting muscles to muscles, *the interplay of muscles*. This totally internal perceptual *tactile* approach reinforced the continuity of motion in movement.

As I came to understand motion through muscles alignment, in contrast to position or visualized line or shape or muscular tonus, I sensed a bridge between technique and feelings. The classic conflict between the body and the spirit without boundaries came to an end. My practical engineering background melded with my romantic idea of *self-expression*. Mother earth came together with Father time through the *tactile* relationship of muscles, emanating the wisp of feelings, rather than images. Sensory consciousness preceded image, eliciting feelings and continuity of motion, rather than thought and associations.

I had finally found a way to teach the kinesthetic experience of dance, to reawaken the sensory experience of motion through muscles. Adult students could begin to perceive where the motion stopped in their musculature, where the connection was non-existent, allowing them to incrementally self-correct misalignments. Their *tactile* perceptual awareness allowed them to alter life-long habits, they didn't even know they were trapped in.

Muscular alignment and feelings are one and the same. This may sound strange since we are so used to separating the sensory experience of feelings from the seemingly totally physical notion of alignment, however, the **silent** *tactile* motion is the same **silent** sensory motion of feelings. This **silent** reality is what resonates within us when we are moved much *before* the words come to register the experience as memory, before the wish to share it with another. **Silence** is the truth of movement as well as the truth of words. If our minds are too busy, if our bodies are too enervated, we do not feel the **silence,** we do not feel.

One student recently called me "Dr. Jack Strangelove." Dr. Strangelove, a character in a Stanley Kubrick film, had a mechanical hand that had a mind of its own. But my association with her use of the name was with a paralyzed arm that would suddenly come alive. Her body was coming alive for her, reawakening itself through the work..... **HOPE**

WALKING
The Call to Freedom

Walking as an opening of our lives
Walking is the birth of a new freedom. It is a momentous event when infants, after crawling for so long, first begin to stand on their own feet. Suddenly, they are above the ground, like a giant among the giants they've been seeing mostly from below. Now they are standing. Before this, only adults – gargantuan

beings who seemed to fly by – could stand and walk and be this way. But now, the toddler is standing. Standing. Despite their wobbly legs, strength surges through their body as muscles tighten around joints for balance. The eyes, already focused ahead, take on novel dimensions as a limitless space opens out. Objects that had been seen mostly from below seem to be closer; a new temporal reality is born with newly found abilities that shrink the distance of objects into sharper focus.

Years later, dirt trails, streets, boulevards, and highways beckon in our dreams of freedom. The paths of our dreams – dreams that have created cars, planes, and the internet – began in our first standing and walking. The space across the floor that had taken so much hand-over-hand movements, with knees scraping and banging, condenses as knees lift and feet announce our presence… walking. Closeness and intimacy are just a few steps away. We no longer were left only able to cry for closeness. We no longer are restricted to chattering for closeness. We can now walk over to them and touch them for intimacy. It is a brave new world.

Do you remember? Does peering down the length of a street remind you? Does driving on a Wyoming highway, with the mountains right in front of you, make you forget that they are hours away? Memory is sensation, fleetingly, passing, shaping associations, shaping history.

The resonance of walking never ends. The freedom of being able to walk away remains an ultimate option in any business transaction. Walking doesn't complete the transaction but our hunger for making a deal doesn't shut off our ability to stand up and walk away. Walking is transitional, the infant becomes a toddler. This is a new identity. One is given new status. Walking changes the child's emotional relationship to the parents, and the parents' relationship with the child. The child can now walk away or towards. They have a new level of mobility, of independence, and will. The parent has to become more watchful because for a child so many crucial boundaries are not visible.

In fact, the demand for freedom continues to have no boundaries. Many people around the world are willing to die for it, to give away the very body that first awakened their longing for freedom. The idea (of freedom) has eclipsed the body in which it was born. The mind becomes the rider and the body the horse. So much comes to fruition with walking. The momentous nature of the event is so far-reaching that it virtually obscures all that came before and led up to it.

The impact of standing and walking on the brain is profound; balance plays a significant role in all our activity. Just look at the pride of a four-year-old on a scooter whizzing by on the sidewalk. You can see three-year-old turning with arms spread out. In their imaginations they may be helicopters rising into the sky. And they tumble down, crashing onto the floor or lawn, giddy with dizziness, only to rise again and again. One day they are doing pirouettes on the ballet stage, on "point," even on one foot. It is amazing what people can learn to do. Circus acrobats doing triple summersaults through the emptiness of space and caught at precisely the right moment by their partners. The beautiful aerialist holding herself by her teeth, twirling so high up we have to strain our necks to see her. Whatever people learn to do that challenges their balance began with their standing and walking.

Any activity that challenges our reflexive sense of balance is often given up on account of the magnitude of the fear that it elicits. Walking is transformative, though we do not recall how powerfully it altered our being when we first learned to stand and walk. The energy of our walk, the length of our stride are reflections of that early experience of freedom or its inhibition. How we walk shows who we are.

Alice walks out on the flat of the heels following my suggested focus. She is so attentive to the flat of the heels that her body remains erect and her neck stiff. She is watchful to comply with my instruction as if by fulfilling my wish she is staying close to me. Still, that sensation of contact with the floor never rises from her feet into her calves. She doesn't exist. Paying attention to the motion rising within her would take her away from her fixation, her maintaining herself through the illusion that she is keeping her contact with the ground and staying close to me by being totally focused on my directive. She remains unconscious of her fixation, what in psychoanalysis is called her transference relation to me. I am, as her teacher, a living image of the parent she dares not move away from lest they become angry or sad. Alice doesn't own her walk. She owns her speech, but not her walk. I have to remind her to sense how the sensation of contact is moving through her feet into her calves, to flex her knees slightly for the motion to go into her thighs, through the pelvis, dropping the lower back, for the motion to move through the torso, relaxing the neck and loosening the head. When she begins owning her walk, she becomes present both physically and emotionally. Everyone in the class marvels at the transformation. The simplicity of it is stunning. Its availability to anyone and everyone, anywhere and at any time is stunning.

Looking at an individual's walk reveals their level of relaxation or tension, whether their body is together or unintegrated, with different parts moving every which way.

We can tell by the pitch of the torso whether their body is coming or going. The walk demonstrates the person's sense of sheer unadulterated presence. When it is totally relaxed their feelings come through as obviously as sunshine filtering through the morning dew.

Suzanne walks out on the flat of the heels squarely touching the ground, the sensation of contact rising through her legs, pelvis, and torso, beautifully. She knows how to follow directions to the letter, there is no resistance. She knows exactly how to do it, as she has always done it. She is conscious of walking out alone, of eyes observing her, creating a tension through her neck that she cannot shake off. This self-consciousness is a fixation, always showing up as a physical tension which, for her, is in the neck. She closes her eyes to block out the eyes of the other adults looking at her. It doesn't work because their eyes and judgments live in her imagination. The tension is beginning to travel down from the neck into her upper back. The tension is building up into an anger, a need to impulsively let go, to not be bound by the imagined others. Observing the physical symptoms of frustration, I decide to remind her to let the weight of her body collapse through the muscles. She easily recalls our working on this in earlier classes and does it perfectly. The tension immediately releases, as the motion initiated by the contact releases the neck, allowing her to walk with unquestionable presence. We again marvel at the transformation. As usual, we're stunned.

As a general principle, the awareness of our weight and the sense of our body mass is the countermeasure to pressure. It is what happens as we go to sleep. We relax our weight. If you feel pressure, release the weight by a long exhalation of the breath. A few exhalations may be necessary.

The importance of this experience cannot be overstated. I believe that all of us retain this implicit sensitivity. We are born with it. It is a birthright. My years of practice have convinced me of the possibility and power of awareness rising from the ruins of suppression: we can all reclaim the tactile sensation through our body walking.

INSTRUCTIONS

Here are simple things to begin with to incorporate the tactile sense of presence into your everyday life:

- Stand **symmetrically** (sensing the same sensation on both feet) over the flat of the heels. Note how this automatically facilitates standing over the **4th toe line** on the sole of the feet, running from the middle of the heels to the ball of the foot of the 4th toe (the toe next to the little toe).
  (Do this incrementally, Do not force.)
- If you're having trouble with the clarity of standing **symmetrically** on both heels, note (by sensing, not looking – just trusting your perception) which foot collapses the arch, even if it is a just little bit collapsed, then bring that leg in, incrementally, closer to the other leg. Play around with how much that leg has to move closer to the other leg until it feels symmetrical.
- You may have to toe-in (incrementally, of course) until the sensation of symmetry of the flat of both heels is, in your sense perception, exactly the same.
- Note which leg is first to respond to the command to take a step. That leg is quicker to contract the muscles

on command because you have habitually favored that leg. It is probably your strongest leg.
- You probably will easily step over the 4th toe line of that foot naturally.
- Now note, as you step out with the other leg, whether it just as easily steps on the 4th toe line of the sole of the foot. It might be a longer stride than the stronger leg. That leg might also swing out away from the center of your body. Just bring that leg closer to the center of the body until you perceive symmetry in your stride. These adjustments should be made as you walk. Keep making these adjustments incrementally. Keep trusting your perception and incremental adjustments. After a while, it begins to feel easy and relaxed because you're not stopping your forward action as you walk.
- Try to step over the 4th toe line on both feet as you walk, making whatever incremental changes you need to make. Every person needs to make different adjustments in different ways. Take your time doing so. Let me re-emphasize that you are educating your muscular perceptions. This takes a special sort of patience.

The typical adjustment to achieve this asymmetry is **narrowing your stance.** Bring the leg taking longer stride in closer to the stronger leg, the one that steps out over the 4th toe line more easily. You have to always return to the symmetry over the flat of the heels. Don't be surprised by what may seem odd, if you need to almost crisscross the longer leg as you walk. You are simply making sure to step over the flat of the heels and 4th toe line. I can assure you that it doesn't take long before you return to a more 'normal' walk and your stride becomes more comfortable. Describing these incremental changes takes a disproportionate amount of effort and time, in contrast to the quickness of our mind and our demand to be have our wishes fulfilled and to have the pain disappear.

(Do this incrementally and comfortably)
- Making these adjustments will correct the slight weakness of the small of the back on the side of the stronger leg. You may have noticed this problem without realizing why or how it was happening.
- By achieving symmetry, you will begin to realign the musculature through your legs and hip insertion, and correct lower back problems. A lot of muscles are readjusting to each other. Patience and respect for the body are essential. Slowly but surely.
- Through **narrowing your stance,** the transference of weight as you walk will be more efficient in the way the motion moves through the musculature of your steps.
- Invariably, staying on the flat of the heels, stepping over the 4th line, and narrowing your stance is going to affect the length of your stride.

(Do this incrementally and comfortably)

Shortening your stride introduces the strongest psychological factor in adjustment, because it affects your 'natural' physical self-assertion. Our **stride** expresses our 'natural' aggression, the force or energy in how we go about doing anything. Take your time sensing how much to adjust the **shortening.** The habituated physical pattern carries a lot of emotional baggage, most of which we've never even thought about, as it begins so early in our development.

- I found out that sliding your foot out slowly from under you into a step is a good way to make sure that you are stepping over the flat of the heels and onto the 4th toe line of the sole of the feet. It has always worked to help people through the transition into what I am suggesting away from the habit of a stride they have been taking for their whole life.
- You are patiently, thoughtfully, respectfully bringing your body in line with your personality until they sync. I suspect that if you are following through on these adjustments, you probably have felt pain and discomfort too often over the years. Or maybe you are one of those adventurous souls willing to try something new to bring body and mind together or, better yet, body and soul in sync.

The humility that comes from learning to respect our psychophysical being can go a long way.

Walking with these incremental adjustments is something to get used to. Believe me when I tell you that it really doesn't take that long to feel totally comfortable with the better alignment that results.

It is only in the immediacy of doing that the benefits of these adjustments can be found. Descriptions, explanations and instructions mean nothing apart from the experience.

Four simple adjustments to make as you walk:

1. Stand symmetrically over the flat of the heels
2. step out onto the 4th toe line of the feet
3. narrow your stance
4. shorten your stride

With every step you take these four adjustments will, slowly but surely, realign the musculature of your legs, pelvis, and lower back. You will in time experience standing and walking as a sense of presence you have probably never imagined.

THE INTERPLAY OF MUSCLES

A practical dance approach to the flow of unconscious feelings

Making the incremental adjustments to perceive the symmetry of sensation on the flat of the heels, and stepping over the 4th toe line of the feet, and narrowing the stance, and shortening the stride: these steps are fairly simple and can be learned by anyone. They require practicing a basic awareness that anyone over the age of ten is capable of. The process of self-correction that these exercises initiate can result in harmful habits falling away. The adjustments are neurologically reconfiguring. The brain automatically begins to release neck and upper back muscles. These muscles have been braced since infancy for support since lifting the head began, an extension of the mother's arms supporting the neck during feedings and rocking.

These adjustments initiate a process of muscular realignment that can release repressed unconscious feelings, especially fear, that have been entrenched in the musculature. The consciousness of motion traveling from the ground through the musculature of the body is like medication. It confirms how a connected musculature is naturally expressive of feelings, not thoughts, but feelings that have not yet reached a thought level. You'll know it by sensing a relaxed body, or by the shedding of tension that may surprise you.

The *interplay of muscles* is the awareness of *tactile* sensation weaving from the contact with the floor through the feet, around the outside of the ankles into the outside muscles of the calves, slowly wrapping around the knees into the back of the thighs and pelvic floor, then rising between the groin and sacrum/lumbar area through the middle of the torso, chest and upper back, passing through the neck and into the fingertips. Describing the progression of the *interplay* gives you some idea of a process of discovery that has to be found incrementally as you go about doing whatever you need to do. I suggest, learning to perceive this progression as you move about, so that it gets integrated functionally, which is how it is supposed to work. Depending on your alignment, your sensitivity to motion within the muscles, and your capacity for so specific an attention, it could take weeks, months or even years. But even the slightest efforts in this direction yield rewards. Once the Interplay of Muscles is established, it continues flowing throughout the body's musculature. Your head will begin to feel lighter as the motion flows through and descends naturally in its continuous *loop* through the musculature. It is a progression of motion that is physically and emotionally surprising. Wordless.

   (Take your time sensing the tactile motion
      as described above)

The biggest trouble, I repeat, is psychological. The process of the Interplay is by its very tactile nature slow, incremental, and very subjective. Our love for speed and immediacy stands in the way of realizing this incredibly available way of living in the body.

We love the immediacy of having our needs met – a waiter appearing to fill our water glass without our having to even ask; the mate who is immediately responsive to the slightest emotional innuendo; the romantic fantasy of love; the speed of our cell phones: the infant in all of us.

Choose whatever activity you are totally familiar with. If the motion of the person's activity moves smoothly throughout the body, chances are that watching them will be almost hypnotic, their work will probably be exquisite, and the person will seem relaxed as they do whatever the work entails. They will probably appear serenely happy, not blissful, just quietly happy.

If they don't function that way and they are simply immersing themselves in their work, frustration ensues and the work suffers; the hand slips, a misstep happens while running, any number of other odd accidents. Injuries then show up, despondency follows with self-questioning, maybe there is drinking too much, or overeating, or some other sort of compensatory self-destructive behavior that flashes the amber light between green and red, telling the person to watch out, slow down, stop.

We normally opt to talk about these emotional rollercoasters in more relational terms. Unhappiness with a husband or wife, or kids, or boss, or society, or…

However, the problem is in our muscular alignment. Some people have it more naturally than others. Most people depend on its instinctual flow, a fortuitous coming together of body, motivation, attention, and so on, what Bernard Malamud celebrated in *The Natural*, his book about a gifted baseball player who Robert Redford portrayed in the movie by the same name.

What I have discovered is teachable. People can learn to slowly realign the musculature, ridding them of all sorts of aches and pains that wear them down.

The following is a dramatic example of the transformative possibility of the Interplay of Muscles.

I've noted this story before, but it definitely highlights the Interplay of Muscles.

He entered the studio, his right leg having an obvious limp as he walked toward me. A 65-year-old, quite tall, lanky, with long white hair pulled back into a ponytail. A professor. He loves dancing. He told me that I was recommended by one of my long-time students and that he would like to join the class.

I told him I was delighted and hoped her recommendation comes true. I mentioned that I had noticed his limp and asked him what the issue was with his right leg.

He said he had had childhood polio when he was six, and that this affected his whole right side. He was so determined for this not to curb his life that he eventually tried out for the track team in high school. It seemed ridiculous but he didn't care. When he got to New York, he even studied modern dance for a number of years.

Given his physical impairment, his enthusiasm was unmistakable. His determination should work in his favor, I thought. The contraction of muscles pulled up and into his right pelvis, affecting the lower back was his private victory over cripple-hood, but it was also the price he paid for his determination. It was not going to be easy to change sixty years of habit and to work with the pride of his determination and achievement which was so embedded in his approach to life.

I was doubtful about succeeding with him. This cautioned me. I told him that my process, though uncomplicated, is slow and long-term. He didn't flinch. He had overcome so many hurdles that it seemed he was prepared both to make the effort and for this not to work.

Fifteen years later, after working with me once a week, he was walking smoothly with an impressive sweep of motion and he was moving to the music without a limp. It was a difficult journey, as he struggled with many of the exercises that he and I tweaked as best we could. What is even more remarkable is the change in his ability to stay within the musculature as he engages his sensitivity to the music.

The emotional evocation of his improvisations began to touch our hearts, even more than his intrepid spirit. The body is no longer the veil of his soul.

In the early 1990s, while teaching a class, I was captivated by another person. During the improvisational part of the class, the student was paying very close attention to never lose the touch contact with the floor, as it rose through her feet and legs, pelvis and torso, releasing the neck as part of the motion, continuing to loop through the body, incrementally – organically.

I become glued watching her feelings floating into space with no intention on her part. The movement from muscles to muscles was seamless, with no breaks, no disconnections, and no aim to be expressive. It was a transcendent experience for me, like the ones I had with Galina Ulanova and with Jeffrey Kern. It was because of her that I began to name the process the *Interplay of Muscles*, because it was like time-lapse photography of petals unfolding. Unbelievable. The simplicity with which her motion was emanating was remarkable.

The progression of the Interplay is a process of sensitizing our perception of motion moving through the tactile texture as we exercise and eventually as we go about doing anything, I mean everything and anything we do in our lives. Again, you can learn to perceive this progression as you move about so that it gets integrated functionally, which is how it is supposed to work. Once the interplay of muscles is sensed, it continues flowing throughout the body's musculature. The head begins to feel lighter as the motion flows through and descends naturally in its continuous loop through the musculature. A sense of motion that is physically and emotionally surprising.

What happens with the interplay sometimes happens for other reasons, at particularly heightened moments or events. The value of the Interplay, I am asserting, is that it is teachable, learnable, practical, personal, organic, self-protective, grounding the body for the multitude of emotions that are unavoidable, by living in the body through which our unconscious flows.

All it requires is our attention.

CHAPTER 7

AWARENESS, THE PRACTICALITY OF PRESENCE

> *I have always tried to render inner feelings
> through the mobility of the muscles*
> ~ Auguste Rodin

What I love about these discoveries that I have made is their practicality.

Becoming conscious of the perception of the symmetry of sensation over the flat of the heels, standing and stepping over the 4th toe line on the sole of the feet, narrowing the distance between the legs to assure clarity in stepping over the flat of the heels and 4th toe line, and ultimately shortening the stride – this affects the psychophysical habit, our physical and emotional being. All of these adjustments can be made as we stand and walk.

These adjustments initiate muscular realignment; they initiate and enhance a perceptual process of bodily awareness that is totally physical; and, over time, they alter lifelong misalignments, the source of aches and pains, by supporting the path for feelings to travel through our body.

The story of Rose comes to mind. Rose always felt unstable. After taking a series of classes, she asked for a private session to deal with her physical discomfort.

She was a smart woman, head of a department at an important hospital. She knew a great deal about psychology. She was amply pear-shaped, which she unconsciously handled by developing too wide a stance. This stance collapsed her arches and contributed to a flat-footed gait that accentuated her shape and also, crucially, her negative body image.

As in many of the examples I have cited, her physical experience was contrary to the speed and lightness of her intellect and her spirit.

She managed to stand over the 4th toe line of her feet, narrowing the distance between her legs to do so. However, her instability remained unchanged. Finding out which leg felt most unstable, gave me the clue to which leg she needed to bring slowly forward to maintain the solidity of the 4th toe line on both feet. There was a seemingly endless series of small, incremental changes, ending with one leg so much more forward than the other leg, and that foot almost pigeon toed, when her voice rose out of the depth of her soul, "This is the first time in my life that I feel stable."

I was utterly surprised by the adjustment we had arrived at. I would never have anticipated it. This was a testament to the individuality of adjustments, to the subjective nature of perceptions. There is no substitute for this personal process.

She was in her early sixties and unlikely to shed the weight that had accumulated over the years. Even if she had done so, the muscular misalignments that had unconsciously developed over time would have remained unchanged.

I can't recall how long she remained in class after this. Bodily experience needs to be *worked through*; it needs to be *practiced*. There are simply too many muscles that need to adjust to each other for realignment to truly hold, to become a comfortable dynamic part of our functioning. My experience has shown me that any changes made in this direction, following these adjustments, are ultimately helpful.

The unusual adjustments that Rose made are an exception to the much smaller adjustments that the vast majority of adults have to make. Most adults simply need to narrow their stance slightly to establish symmetry of sensation over the 4th toe line placement, with the toes of one foot needing to swivel in, just a tiny bit, to achieve symmetry on both feet For some, the toes on both feet need to swivel in. Swiveling is always incremental and subjectively dictated.

Symmetry and incremental adjustments are, again, the principles for how to exercise to reach re-alignment of the musculature. Everyone is built and perceives sensation differently.

Practicality is the only way to function incrementally, to initiate walking over the 4th toe line placement – the one and only placement that facilitates the muscular resonance of motion from the floor through the body to the neck, the only placement that strengthens the muscles pumping blood in the arteries back up to the heart.

Incremental adjustments and perception of symmetry makes achieving one's ideal posture practical and dynamic by keeping the motion through the muscles alive.

Practicality is the unadorned poetry of dance. The unifying process between mind and body.

Practicality is hope in action.

PRESENCE

> *"Nothing ever becomes real 'til it is experienced."*
> ~ John Keats

Laura thrusts her right arm out like a thunderbolt, with a harsh flattened palm, momentarily freezing the body, then sharply retracting the arm as her palmed hand slowly wipes her face. She's bending head and torso towards the ground, then unexpectedly lifts a leg behind into a majestic sweeping turn, ending in a silenced body. She has always been proud of her long legs and the skill she's acquired.

Her impressive command of her impulses – feelings bolt out of her body like instincts – has elicited admiration from the class. The combination of improvisational freedom and controlled skill always evokes a sense of wonder from all those less skilled and less free in their exhibitionism.

She has repeated aspects of this sequence of gestures over the course of forty plus years. Forty years with about forty-four classes a year (that's about 1,760 classes) of demonstrating a movement sequence of incredible personal import. She is so unquestionably trusting in her internal flow of impulses that it has been very difficult to affect the repetition of her gestures. There has always been a profound individualistic streak in the way she followed instructions, as if she has been saying "I know my body. I know it so intimately that I need to do what you asked for in just this way." It's not that I haven't tried to assert my authority by making clear my reasoning and concerns. Other members of the class have also, in a less concerted way, have brought attention to her repetitions, but nothing has ever had an effect on their eventual reappearance.

It made me angry in the past when I was more invested in my authority. But in time, I accepted Laura's resistance. I had learned enough over the years to know that how she was had a lot to do with her mother, who had a very competitive streak. But that, by itself, doesn't really tell us very much about her personal need to sustain a particular emotional stance that only a movement sequence could express. I've thought of that sequence as her allegorical statement of self – a silent protest for all to see. The self-protective need of her gestural repetition became obvious in the sense that the quickness of her sudden gestures and dominance of the space simply said, "Don't get too close." I can't recall that she ever shed light on that pattern.

What is it about movement and bodily patterns that seem to have such a hold?

You might think that the answer is simple. The infant is brought to the areola around the nipple and usually begins at two sucks per second for ten to twenty minutes. Habits actually begin in the womb. The transmissions from mother to fetus are basically predispositions to foods, smell, taste, sound, and rhythms, that usually show up chemically and mentally postnatally and, most impressively, later in life according to research showing how the brain registers experience in the fetus.

The kind of repeated muscular experience in the complex process of feeding, the touch, the quality of support, the meeting and closeness of the eyes, the moving towards and away from all contribute powerfully to the formation of our muscular sensibility.

The body, specifically the musculature, is the recipient and the carrier of this pattern of repetitions. We refer to these powers as body memory. These are so physically and emotionally embedded that they can negate our intention, even though we are in principle capable of following our intentions. Our aims are simply undermined, affecting our sense of control, maybe heightening our determination or making us give up, or hopefully making us realize that there are unconscious determinants. As a movement teacher, it has always amazed me how some people have minimal body memory, as if the body comes and goes with no continuity.

What starts off as a positive body to mind connection in our infancy can become a psychological roadblock. Laura's predisposition to battle my efforts to impact on her imaged sense of her body is a perfect example of a psychological roadblock. She eventually adopts a correction I give after months, sometimes even years after I offered it.

Habits both physical and mental are difficult to influence. I know this full well as an improvisational dance teacher and as a psychoanalyst. We hold on for dear life to our repetitions, our imitations, security blankets from the past – mother, womb, a longing for return, for non-existence, an imaginary absence of problems. We all know that security blankets are substitutes for the real thing – mommy, the real source of security. Our security blankets are increasingly more sophisticated in how they mask and distance us from the source of our fears – our feelings. They mask our frightening need of the person upon which we were so dependent, they mask our fear of separation, our fear of loss.

The iconic Orson Welles film, *Citizen Kane* comes to mind, when Kane with his dying breath whispers, "'Rosebud' – the trade name of a cheap little sled on which Kane was playing on the day he was taken away from his home and his mother. In his subconscious it represented the simplicity, the comfort and, above all, the lack of responsibility in his home, and it also stood for his mother's love which Kane never lost."[13] His subsequent fame and power could not substitute for the memory of his childhood and this maternal embrace of safety and freedom.

We are born to absorb indiscriminately the maternal embrace. Regardless of our best efforts to kill that aspect of the self, it continues to function, whether we acknowledge it or not.

The fear of loss is not only of the love object, the mother, the source of safety, but of the mind that organizes that truth, and the loss of the body that houses that mind.

The fear of loss of the body, which most of us have unconsciously repressed, comes up more often with women who have to confront menses on a monthly basis for many years of their life. Even when the transition is smooth, anticipated, and prepared for, it is consequential. Women don't have a monopoly on this fear, but they generally do worry about their body more than men. And our cultures reinforce that preoccupation, often in unhealthy ways.

When the negation of the body emerges, as in suicide or in masochistic behaviors, it harbors a dangerous turning point in consciousness, in our capacity to deal with separation and the sadness of loss implicit in separations. The body is not simply our sense of being alone, it is presence. Negation of the body suggests a mind floating away into an imaginary belief that the body is not necessary, a mind intoxicated by its associations and images. There is maybe a hierarchy of food, mother, body-self, psychological self, but psychologically these are indistinguishable or interchangeable. And this confusion of

---

13 Partial quote from a press statement by Orson Welles on January 15, 1941 prior to the release of the film by RKO.

identity is central to how proceeding as if control equals safety seems to work for most people.

Food and sex are fundamental to our survival. They are generators of life and continuity. The place food and sex have in our lives has decisive social meanings. They are fields for what is acceptable or marginal. We can improvise to enliven these areas of our lives when they become boring and curb them when they become threatening. But we seldom consider what makes food and sex so incredibly important and so full of variations and conflicts.

Since food is necessary for survival, isn't it reasonable to suspect that it becomes unconsciously symbolic of our fear of death? It makes sense that food and death are fundamentally bound. It suggests that eating too much is indicative of an unconscious but never totally repressed fear of emptiness – of death. Does the anorexic defy the repressed fear of death, of non-existence by not allowing hunger? Recognizing the intimate associations of food, body, and mother can help us understand overwhelming feelings of self-doubt. In anguish, depression, fear, and anger there is a core impression that we are not sensed; to not be seen or related to can leave us with the sense that we don't exist. These are not uncommon feelings in the process of growing up, varying in intensity depending on the experience of loss, especially love.

Do we defy our fear of death, our fear of not being, by curbing our appetites? Does the anorexic person stand at the precipice, screaming with their body until we are left trembling, looking at the skeletal creature, death? Do we live entering, encompassing symbolically in sex, like the initial experiences of infancy – nipple enters, mouth opens, muscles suck, silencing the abdominal spasms of death?

The amalgam of food, mother, and body is an unconscious template and makes for a multitude of creative possibilities. Consider the notion of the male as the mother entering, and the woman as the infant being entered; or the woman straddling, enters the awaiting male erection; or the teacher enters, the student is entered; the coach excites, the players feed; the boss dictates, the employee executes. Endless variations on a template we function so basically with. We think of the centrality of identity issues with teenagers and how these are associated with the fear of death. Their dreams, anxieties, and daring-do engagements. The French refer to the orgasm as the Petite Mort (the little death). We are psychically transformed in the act of sex by a union beyond the body through the body. Is the connection of food and death an unacknowledged driving force of purpose, fulfillment, of orgasm, and destiny? The body is always needed, even to die.

I bring up these possibilities to show the movement from body to mind, then from above to below, from mouth to genitals. To consider this instinctual body-based, generative, sensory process can be dizzying and deeply disturbing. We are so inclined to believe our mind controls, to consider otherwise can be downright enraging. It can puncture the mostly unconscious fantasy that our mind gives us safety – that our mind is safety.

To consider the body-as-mind has implications for our notion that our psychological life is totally determined by the people that have raised us and shaped us. This is not to dismiss the profound influence of our parents on our character. Nevertheless, the body (specifically the musculature, the internal carrier of love and hate by its contractive nature and function) cannot be left out of the equation of behavioral determinants, of character, of personal choices; most importantly, the body is a communication from beyond our consciousness. I remind you of Laura's silent endlessly recurring movement pattern.

I am reminded of the nursery rhyme, Humpty Dumpty.

Humpty Dumpty sat on a wall.
Humpty Dumpty had a great fall.
All the king's horses and the king's men
Could not put Humpty Dumpty together again.

Do we fall off the wall when food and sex lose their attraction? When core realities dissipate, separating inside from outside? We ask questions about the depressed, "Are they still interested in eating? Are they responsive to affection, to touch?" We are impressed by the primal expressions of the wish to live, the engagement with survival – the **body** and **presence**.

Patterns, repetitive bodily movement patterns are bound to a generative source – survival.

Let me share with you the unanticipated resolution of this seemingly unavoidable divide between body and mind, between inside and outside, that surprised me, and continues to this day to shock me.

The initiation of the flat of the heels exploration, which in turn supported the earlier tactile interplay of muscles, and reinforced the 4th toe line alignment of the sole of the feet, culminating in the loop of motion throughout the body… This dissolved Laura's repetitive pattern of isolating a part of the body, the definitive open-palm arm gesture, the sequence that seemed so unyielding, disappeared without Laura's having a conscious intention or resolve to change.

Observing the disappearance of this gestural pattern that had lasted for over forty years was psychologically shocking. How did it happen? How does it continually happen that repetitive patterns evaporate without intention, not just for Laura, but for every person in class? There is no effort to control the unconscious emergence of movement, of gestures, of shapes. The attention to the tactile loop of motion gives the impression of total presence.

Presence, the unadorned flow of feelings through the musculature is a natural expression.

I meditate on why the *loop* initiated *by the flat of the heels*, into *the interplay of muscles* has so remarkable an effect. Why do movement patterns, deep and lifelong habits, naturally dissipate in the improvisations of these mature adults? Mary, another adult student tells me that her awareness of the Interplay walking her dogs makes an incredible difference in how she lives her day.

Does the *looping muscular interplay* merge *inside and outside*? Does it merge heart and body so fully in the **NOW** that iconic expressions of identity (in the form of symbolic movement displacements) are no longer needed to express a profound generative connection to survival? Is the *present* so powerfully activated by this *loop of motion* through the musculature that these habitual symbolic expressions become less insistent? Does the sensitivity to our tactile motion quietly express the survival of the feeling self?

Movement patterns are memory, somaticized psychological defenses of a primal sensitive part of the self. *The interplay of muscles* allows this non-verbal sensibility to flower physically as a dance, sometimes without any breaks, sometimes with minor retractions. It feels remarkable to observe and to resonate empathically, even though we have no intention of doing this, as if this is our innate legacy, this is what is in-born (or hard-wired – in the techie idiom of our culture), available to each one of us. We are connected.

With Laura, as with all long-time students improvising with this focus, there is not the slightest inkling of trying to transform. Change happens by virtue of the very specific focus on the flat of the heels and looping interplay of muscles that facilitates a continual flow of organically changing gestures and shapes, physically and emotionally.

It seems to me as simply a natural physical expression of feelings, neither more nor less. We sense and dance our unconscious.

This is our endowment. Own it. Let its grace happen. Hope is the light of presence.

CODA

I began with the story of my father, with his secret for remaining engaged in living, despite the abandonments he experienced early in life and the fears that went along with these early losses. His optimism helped him to deal with the physical and cognitive impairment of his last years in the nursing home. His retort to me, "You never know what is going to happen tomorrow," encapsulated his reversal of fear and anger, a way to live out the silence in his body.

I sensed his secret as a child before he put it so clearly into words over tea and cookies. His secret loomed ever larger in my inner life, helping me to deal with my own fears, and eventually bursting forth in my resolve to become an artist. In hindsight, my choice memorializes the aloneness of abandonment that I sensed about him and myself so many years ago.

Throughout the years of creating, of dancing, then acting, and eventually directing theater, founding a school, and then becoming a practicing psychoanalyst, and all the rewards of public recognition, I maintained the separate observing eye of aloneness, a guarded self.

Teaching creative movement for over fifty years has taught me that my separate body is an illusion. The awareness of the Interplay of Muscles made me realize that the body is a dynamic system that joins all of us to everything around us. By perceiving the tactile flow of motion and the connected relationship of muscles, the body realigns. It happens slowly, facilitating motion that creates a distinct dance each time, ever anew – the dance of our unconscious. The awareness exposed every hidden aspect of my created separate self, to discover the constancy of feelings passing through me like the lapping waters on a beach.

My father's curiosity steadied my journey. Movement, as I talk about it, dissolves the imaged separate body, enlivening our connectedness as presence, as being, and being as hope.

Presence is neither more nor less. It is.

BIO

Principle movement training in Modern Dance with Jose Limon, Martha Graham, Merce Cunningham, Alwin Nikolais and Murray Lewis, Lester Horton; technique with Jimmy Truitte; Ballet: Alfredo Corvino, Antony Tudor, Julia Baraskova; Afro-

Cuban: Telly Beatty; Choreography: Doris Humphrey, Louis Horst, Lucas Hoving, Helen Tamiris; Music with Norman Lloyd; Idiokenisis with Lulu Sweigard; Labanotation with Ann Hutchinson; Dance aesthetics with Otto Ludwig Binswanger; Lighting with Tom Skelton and Gary Smith. Danced with the Fred Berk modern/folk dance company for three years. Pick-up concerts with Yemima Ben-Gal, Charles Weidman, and Felix Fibich. Made the audition cut from 250 to 25 for West Side Story movie, with Jerry Robbins making the final decisions. Acted with the Yiddish Folksbiene Theater for two seasons. The only featured actor in Bruce Davidson's documentary film, *"Isaac Singer's Nightmare and Mrs. Pupko's Beard."* The first Teacher-in-Charge of the Adult Performing and Creative Arts Evening Community Center at P.S. 199 for the Board of Education. Mr. Wiener taught movement for actors, and theater directing at Richmond College, CUNY, in Staten Island, and was an Adjunct Assistant Professor at Hunter College, CUNY, in the graduate department. He directed the world premieres of an operetta, *Gimple, the Fool,* based on the story by Nobel Laureate I. B. Singer; the one and only mystery play by Martin Buber, *Elijah,* for Manhattanville College of the Sacred Heart, reviewed by the former lead reviewer of the Herald Tribune, Walter Kerr, *"Professional theater comes to Westchester."* The premier production for the 92nd "Y" Children Theater Program, *Solomon and Ashmedai,* based on a poem by Chaim N. Bialik with an original score and lyrics by Doris Schwerin and Rhoda Bellak.

The publication of *Creative Movement for Children: A Dance Program for the Classroom,* (1969) co-authored with John Lidstone, Ph. D., brought international recognition to the School for Creative Movement founded in 1962.

Anatole Broyard, a celebrated New York Times columnist and editor of the Book Review wrote *"It's your Move,"* about his movement experience with Mr. Wiener, *"My wife who is a dancer and several of her dancer friends described him as someone who not only changed and improved the way they moved, he had also altered the way they felt themselves to exist."*

Published, *The Way of the 4th Toe: Into the Feeling Body,* (2011).

Mr. Wiener, founder and co-director of the School for Creative Movement, (1962–1992), is a New York State licensed psychoanalyst in private practice in Manhattan. He continues to teach one adult movement class. *jawiener6@gmail.com*

www.ingramcontent.com/pod-product-compliance
Lightning Source LLC
Chambersburg PA
CBHW072004110526
44592CB00012B/1198